beautiful things.

a memoir.

Kaylie Walkington

beautiful things.
a memoir.

Kaylie Walkington

Beautiful Things. A Memoir.

The Pink Goldfish Co.

ISBN-13: 978-0-692-99208-1

Edited by Ashley Alexander
Cover and Interior Design by Kaylie Walkington
Formatting by Michael Walkington

Follow me on Facebook:
https://www.facebook.com/beautifulthingsmemoir

Email me at: beautifulthingsmemoir@gmail.com

Printed in the United States of America
First Printing: February 2018

The Pink Goldfish Co.

Pink Goldfish

dedication.

This book is dedicated to all those who supported us during the trial of our lives. To those who sent cards, gifts, and encouraging messages through text and our Facebook Page, "Pray for Kaylie." To those who helped financially, who made us meals, and who babysat our kids. To Mike's employers who were flexible and generous, and to the students who organized an incredible baby shower for our little boy, Tug.

I want to thank my doctors and everyone else on my care team. Not only did they work tirelessly to treat my illness, but also to brighten my days. Their dedication to save lives, and especially mine, is something I will always admire.

We are so grateful for our parents, family, and friends and for the countless hours they sacrificed to travel and be with us in Seattle. We're grateful for their undying, unconditional love and support.

I am so grateful for my friend and editor, Ashley Alexander, who worked so hard to help me edit this book and tell my story. Her editing skills were incredible, but her loving heart is even greater. Without her, this story would be incomplete.

I am especially thankful for Mike, for his pure and loving heart, his unlimited compassion, his positivity, and his strength. Thank you, my darling. I couldn't have made it without you. I dedicate this book to you and our beautiful babies, Zoey and Tug. May you all know how deeply I love you.

Lastly, I want to thank our Father in Heaven, for it is because of Him that I am here to write this story. I thank Jesus for walking alongside me during this incredible trial. Even in the darkest times, He was always there.

contents.

introduction.

I've always loved to write. Somewhere in my storage unit is a box of various journals: a blue, plain notebook from second grade, a black-papered one filled with junior high dreams written with fancy gel pens, and the latest turquoise one in which I write letters to God. I have online journals that I used to write in while it was slow at work. Now I have a journal app on my phone that I try to write in daily.

During college, I started a personal blog. I wrote about day-to-day happenings and thoughts. While some of the things I've written now seem silly, other entries have given me insight years later.

Writing has always been a form of therapy for me, a safe place to analyze and hopefully make some sense of this crazy thing we call life. Naturally, when the worst happened, I turned to writing to deal with it. As I wrote, I felt the overwhelming need to share my story, so I created the blog "Pregnant with Lymphoma," which became the foundation of this book.

So here it is: my story. I can't believe that I can say this now, but I am grateful for it. It is a part of me, and I wouldn't be the person I am without the experiences I've had.

In February 2015, I was twenty-six weeks pregnant with my son when I was diagnosed with cancer. The diagnosis, treatments, procedures, and sickness threatened to overcome me. I almost lost my baby boy. I was flooded with emotions I had never felt: true fear and deep sadness; pure joy and gratitude; so much pain and sickness. I came very close to death but also experienced miracles firsthand. During this enormous trial, I witnessed some of the most beautiful things.

My hope is that my story will show you what I learned:

We are deeply loved children of an amazing God, and even in our darkest hours, the Lord, our Savior, Jesus Christ is there in our midst. I can say without a doubt that God is good. He walked with me through the worst part of my life, and I will always be grateful for the relationship that cancer developed between us.

This is a story of the amazing generosity of friends, family, and strangers. A story that tells of incredible things ordinary people did to help me and my family. I hope that as you read you too feel the love that I have felt, and that you understand how truly incredible and tremendously loved you are. I also hope you will be able to see the miracles that are all around you.

Things don't always turn out the way we want them to, but I believe that the story God writes for our lives is always greater than what we can write for ourselves.

This is the story He wrote with my life.
It is my prayer that you too will experience
peace, hope and grace
in the story God is writing for you.

CHAPTER ONE

pregnant with lymphoma.

"For I know the plans I have for you," declares the Lord, "plans to prosper you and not to harm you, plans to give you hope and a future."

-Jeremiah 29:11 NIV

When I was diagnosed with cancer, I was a young wife to my high school sweetheart Mike, mother to our three-year-old daughter, Zoey, and twenty-six weeks pregnant with our son, Tug. Never in my life had I ever dealt with something so big, and I was scared out of my mind.

Up until that point I had a rough but normal pregnancy, which included a lot of morning sickness and a real struggle to eat anything. I thought it was strange that I hadn't gained a single pound, especially since I gained over forty with my first baby. However, the baby was growing fine, and I was told not to worry. I was tired, short of breath, my face was swollen, it was hard for me to eat, and my shoulders hurt when I was sleeping—all normal pregnancy symptoms according to the pregnancy websites. I dealt with these symptoms for over two months, believing that it was caused by my pregnancy. However, I started to feel dizzy and weak. I couldn't stand up for more than a minute before I felt like I was going to faint. On Super Bowl Sunday of 2015, Mike took me to Urgent Care, thinking maybe I had pneumonia or something. My heart rate was 160 bpm, and the doctor, fearing that I had a pulmonary embolism (a blood clot in my lung), sent me to the ER at Evergreen Hospital. I was concerned at that moment but still felt as though things would be okay.

At the ER they rushed me right in since the doctor at Urgent Care had called ahead. Within an hour, I had received an electrocardiogram and a computed tomography (CT) scan, which showed my heart was in distress. When the results came back, the doctors gathered in my room and explained that there was too much fluid around my heart and a large tumor in my chest. I could hear what the doctors were saying, but it felt like I was in a weird dream—an awful nightmare. I did everything I could not to have a panic attack, but when I saw the CT scan my heart sank. I just couldn't believe this was real.

While all of this was happening, Mike was busy taking care of Zoey. When the doctors told him I was headed to the Catheterization Lab to drain the fluid around my heart, (a procedure nicknamed a "heart tap,") and would be in the hospital for a couple of days, he called our friends, and they were there to pick up Zoey within twenty minutes. Saying goodbye to my daughter was the first time I really broke down. I gave her a tight hug, a kiss on her cheek, and Mike took her out to the car. As soon as he came back the doctors whisked me away towards the Cath Lab. They were in such a hurry and pushing me so fast that I had to ask them to stop and let me say goodbye to Mike. We exchanged sad smiles, he gave me a quick hug, and off I went.

They took me into the procedure room, rolling my ER bed next to the hard, thin operating table. People were running around, opening supplies, setting up the instruments and sterile equipment that would be needed. They had me lie on my right side, pulled up my gown, and prepped my left chest area with cold antiseptic liquid. Next came the blue surgical drapes, covering my entire body except my face and the area that had been prepped.

The cardiologist came into the room, was gowned and gloved by the surgical tech, and stepped up to my side. They gave me a sedative, and as it hit my brain, I felt instantly relaxed. I talked with the doctor as he used an ultrasound machine to analyze my heart. I joked with the tech that I was watching him, and I made sure to let him know that I used to be a surgical technologist too, and he better not mess up. I can imagine that he thought I was annoying, as he was trying to do his job in a stressful situation.

When the doctor was done scanning, he described how

my right atrium was "angry" and not even pumping. I would find out later that this was called cardiac tamponade, a life-threatening condition. The 23cm x 15cm lymphoma tumor had pushed up against my heart to the point that it blocked the fluid that surrounding my heart in the pericardial sac from draining, causing a condition called pericardial effusion. They pulled the X-ray machine over and took a few scans. The doctor told me that the next part was not going to be fun, and he was right.

After finding the right spot, he took a long needle that was attached to a plastic catheter tube and pierced me with a very long needle, through my ribs, straight into my chest. As the needle was rotated and positioned inside, I sobbed, in excruciating pain. The sedative had kept me calm until this point, but it was no longer enough.

He finally got it in the correct spot, pulled the needle out, leaving the catheter, and began draining the fluid in my pericardial sac. I watched the empty bag hanging next to me fill as he pulled one syringe out at a time. The fluid looked bloody, and the bag continued to fill up until it reached the 800mL mark. I had monitors strapped on my belly the entire time, monitoring Tug's every move. An obstetric doctor stood, watching intensely, protecting my baby as I underwent this awful procedure.

Mike was in the waiting room during the procedure. He said he knew how serious it was when he saw the nurses roll out the emergency C-section supply cart and leave it by the door. It still makes me sad to think of how scared he was waiting outside that procedure room.

After the heart tap I was taken to the Critical Care Unit, where the nurses quickly worked to place IVs. My tumor was blocking major blood vessels in my chest, as well as collapsing parts of my lung, trachea, and esophagus. Because it was obstructing so many vital passageways, the care team was concerned about placing an IV in my arm, so they called in the best nurses in the hospital to place one in my foot. It took them seven tries to finally get an IV in and because the foot is full of nerves, it was extremely painful. Mike held my hand and talked me through it as I wept. I could not have gotten through it without his help.

The first night in the hospital our team of nurses and doctors worked to stabilize me. They told Mike and I to sleep, an impossible task when there was so many thoughts and worries racing through our heads. We were so scared and felt paralyzed with fear. We spent the night crying and praying together, having no clue what the morning would bring.

Looking back on the situation, I can see miracles in the middle of all the fear and chaos. First, I made it to the ER in time. If I would have gone into cardiac arrest at home, I couldn't have made it. Second, the ER doctor working that night knew exactly what to do and what tests to order, making it possible for him to quickly figure out the problem. Because I had worked in the medical field since I was eighteen, I knew that medicine is not an exact science and that I could have been easily misdiagnosed in the ER and sent home. I'm still alive today because everything fell into place on that terrifying night, and for that I will always be grateful.

CHAPTER TWO

goodbyes.

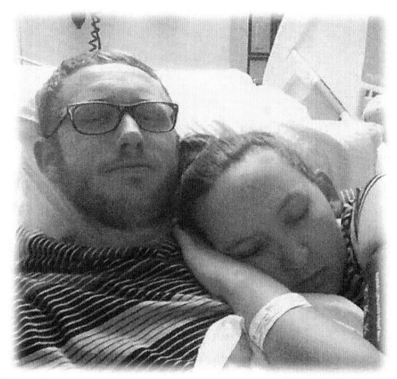

"And now these three remain: faith, hope, and love. But the greatest of these is love."

1 Corinthians 13:13 — NIV

At four in the morning on my first night in the hospital, my oncologist came into my room to tell me that she was pretty sure I had Primary Mediastinal B-Cell Lymphoma. A tissue biopsy confirmed the diagnosis later that day. She explained that I would need a certain type of chemotherapy called DA-EPOCH-R, and it was safe to do while I was pregnant, which amazed me! This type of cancer had a great prognosis with a ninety-five percent cure rate.

However, what she, the cardiologist, hospitalist, and especially the ICU anesthesiologist were concerned about was that the cancer had spread into my heart and vessels, and that as I received treatment, a hole could potentially develop in my heart—a possibility she described as "catastrophic." I had well over twenty doctors working on my case, and every specialist in the Seattle area was consulted. The look of worry in each of their faces as they came into my room frightened us. As they all described the scenario that could occur, where the chemo basically melted away my heart, the fear became unbearable.

At one point, my obstetrician and her team came in. They explained that because the tumor was blocking my vessels and collapsing my lung, trachea, and esophagus, I was too unstable to operate on, and if something happened to the baby, they would not be able to save us both. Then they posed the worst question I've ever been asked: "Kaylie, if it comes down to it and your baby is in distress, do we save you, or do we save your baby?"

Faced with the possibility that I wouldn't even make it through chemotherapy because my heart might melt away with the tumor, I had to decide who they were going to save—me or my unborn child. Mike was sitting next to me, holding my hand, and when I looked over at him, he had tears in his eyes. He said, "Kaylie, Zoey and I need you. I don't want to lose our baby, but I can't lose you." With that, I knew my decision, but to hear it come out of my mouth was eerie. As a mother, saying that I would rather live than save my unborn baby felt wrong. But I also knew that I needed to be here to be a mother to my daughter and a wife to my husband. It was a decision I would never wish on anyone—it was horrible.

After that horrible talk, they stopped monitoring my baby and focused their care on me. They explained that if something did happen to him and he passed, they would wait until I was stable to deliver him. The fear and worry I felt were immeasurable.

That first night, when Mike and I were finally alone for a minute, we just held each other and wept. We both felt that I wasn't going to make it through the week, and we spent the night saying goodbye. We cried as we talked about how blessed we had been over the last ten years to have had such an amazing relationship. We have always felt that what we had was special because even though we have had our fights, we've always been each other's best friend. We said how lucky we were to have met at sixteen, gotten married at nineteen, and to have built such a wonderful life together with our beautiful little girl. I made him promise that he would be happy again, fall in love, and have a family. He promised me he would make sure Zoey knew who I was and what I believed. And he told me how much he loved me. We once again tried to sleep, but our hearts were too heavy. Instead we just held hands, me in the hospital bed, him in the recliner, as we tried to make it through the worst night of our lives.

I am incredibly grateful that we made it through that first week, and despite all the odds, that I made it out of the ICU alive. I am so grateful that Mike and I have no regrets. Even in the moment we thought we were going to lose each other, all we needed to say were words of love and gratitude.

We still worried that something could go wrong in my treatment, and fearful that there were still many unknowns. However, we also knew that life is fragile, and anyone's can be taken away in a second. We learned that to live in fear is crippling, and our job is to live each day as if it is our last, full of faith, trusting God in every moment of every day. I learned that even though fear would always be lurking in the darkness, that I would have the strength to overcome it. I felt truly blessed for my life and the people in it, and that because of their love, everything would be okay.

CHAPTER THREE

He was there.

"Fear thou not; for I am with thee: be not dismayed; for I am thy God: I will strengthen thee; yea, I will help thee; yea I will uphold thee with the right hand of my righteousness."

-Isaiah 41:10 KJV

On my second day in the ICU, the doctors told me I would undergo many procedures and tests that would be very painful. With so much to grapple with in such a short time, Mike and I were so upset that we felt like we couldn't make it through the day. We asked to talk to the social worker, and she came and helped us work through the feelings that were preventing us from moving forward so we could start treatment. We tried to explain, through sobs, the fear of me dying was too much to bear. We were so terrified, we didn't know how we could make it through the week. The social worker gave us the best advice, saying, "Don't look at the big picture if it's too overwhelming. Your job is just to focus on the next minute, hour, or day...whatever you can handle. Just take one step at a time."

After she left, we said another prayer together and felt filled with enough courage to face the day. My dad and Mike's mom arrived from Utah to help support us. Up until their arrival, two close friends were taking care of Zoey for us. Having good friends is always important, but even more so in a crisis. We are grateful that even though we didn't have any family in Seattle, we had incredible friends who stepped in. However, having our parents there was a huge relief, and I know we could not have made it through the first week without them. We've always felt blessed with wonderful families and friends but seeing everyone pull together to help us was a testament to that. They lifted us up, supported us, and encouraged us.

I had many painful procedures done throughout my second day in the hospital. First, I had a tissue biopsy done on the tumor, which included placing a six-inch needle in my chest. Next, I had a bone marrow biopsy performed, which was by far the most painful thing I had ever experienced. The biopsy is done by drilling out part of the hip bone to get into the bone marrow. Lastly, I had a PICC line (a plastic tube inserted directly into larger, more central veins) placed in my groin, which would be used the next day for the chemotherapy. Because they were so worried about my airway, they couldn't give me much sedative, so I was very awake during the procedures. Thankfully, they let Mike stay in the room with me, and he held my hand during all of it. I cried a lot, but holding my love's hand, listening to him encourage me, and seeing his face gave me strength. The little bit of sedative they could give me made me a bit loopy, and during the procedure I told Mike, "I think I just saw a cat! Shhh…don't tell anyone!" He laughed, and so did I.

Later that day, they did an MRI to see if there were any other tumors present in my body. Even though I am not claustrophobic, I was terrified to have the imaging done because the tumor made it impossible to lie on my back and breathe normally. This made things complicated during the MRI when they would ask me repeatedly for over forty-five minutes to hold my breath for up to twenty seconds, each time causing me to cough violently. They explained that they knew I couldn't do it, but that I had to do my very best to hold still so they could get a good image.

They wrapped me up in blankets, put me on the narrow board, and placed plastic boards on top of me. I was asked what type of music I wanted, and I chose to listen to Joshua Bell, one of my favorite violinists. I used to listen to him when I studied, and his music always calmed me down. Next thing I knew, I was being pushed into the tiny tunnel, and I could feel the panic rising. Even though the other procedures were painful, this was the most terrifying thing I had been through yet. Not being able to breathe and being stuck in a small space was absolutely horrifying, and I could feel the tears running down my face. One of my favorite ICU nurses sat at the head of the machine and stroked my hair the entire time. Even though it helped, I started praying and didn't stop until the forty-five minutes were up.

In that MRI, I prayed and begged for the Savior to be with me, to comfort me, and to help me. I prayed for my family, that if something did happen to me, they would be okay and feel comforted. I prayed that a miracle would occur, and that despite all the odds, I would be able to fight this cancer, get my baby boy here safely, and have more time with my family on earth. Up until this point in my life, I had never been at a place where I felt like I was at the end of my rope and that I had nothing left to rely on but God. I had never fully needed Him until now, and through my tearful prayers, *He was there.*

A couple of months before this happened, Mike and I were driving home from church, enjoying the evergreen tree-lined highway, listening to our "Sunday Mix," when the song "Oceans" by Hillsong United came on.

The lyrics talk about how Jesus asks us to follow Him out into the ocean, where things are tumultuous and unsure, and to places we feel uncomfortable in. However, during extreme turmoil, caught in fierce oceans waves,

Jesus is there. When we are terrified beyond belief, we need to let ourselves trust in His love, knowing that He will rescue us.

I have loved this song since the day I first heard it. I spent my childhood with my family on the water, either boating at Utah's beautiful Flaming Gorge reservoir or on the sandy beaches of North Carolina. Water has always had a special place in my heart, and when I heard this song, I felt like it was written especially for me.

As we listened in the car that day, we talked about how we hoped we would have a chance to experience a situation in our lifetime where we had to completely rely on God and let faith carry us. We had prayed for such an experience, where we could truly know and feel God's embrace, to be the recipients of Grace, and to truly need Him. Suddenly we found ourselves in the middle of the "ocean," calling upon His name and finding ourselves in the presence of our Savior.

Before cancer, I was standing on the sandy beach, admiring the beauty and majesty of the ocean. Afterwards, I found myself so far out in the water, that my feet were no longer touching the ground, and I was afraid. This song played repeatedly in my mind, giving me hope that I would survive. It reminded me to keep my focus on Jesus, trusting that his Grace would rescue me, and bring me back to shore.

As the test results came in, the positive news gave us hope. First, we found out that the pericardial fluid showed no cancer cells, which meant that the chance of the chemotherapy harming my heart was very unlikely. Next, the MRI showed that the cancer was only in my chest. Lastly, the bone marrow results came back clean, showing that the cancer had not metastasized. We slowly but surely started crawling out of that deep, dark, hopeless despair we had found ourselves in during the first forty-eight hours in the hospital, and into a place of renewed hope and optimism.

The preliminary MRI results gave the doctors a better idea of what was going on with me. They could see how big the tumor really was, how much my lungs and trachea were being squashed, and that both of my jugular veins were blocked with giant blood clots. Once they felt it was safe enough, they started treatment.

I began chemo on the third day in the ICU. Two nurses walked into my room, double and triple verifying that I was indeed Charlotte Kaylie Walkington and that my date of birth was correct. They gowned up, put on two pairs of gloves, and covered their faces with a mask and googles. They showed me the bag of chemo, covered in yellow hazard stickers, and hung it up on my IV pole. Before beginning, the oncologist came into the room, verifying once again, that this poison was for me. They connected the chemo to my PICC line, and the red tinted fluid slowly flowed through the plastic tube into my veins.

It was very strange, but we were all very excited for it to begin. Knowing that this drug was going to kill that nasty tumor was a relief. The doctor told me that this type of cancer "melts like butter" with chemo, and that I would shortly feel the effects. I was surprised that I did not feel nauseous right away. I was even more surprised as the hours and days went by that I could feel my lungs popping open, and I could sleep lying flat again now that the tumor and the fluid was not squashing everything inside. My cough, my breathing, and the nerve pain in my arms all quickly improved. It was such a relief that the poisonous medicine could make me feel better. Amazingly, my placenta blocked it from reaching my son, protecting his precious life.

While we don't believe that my cancer was a blessing, the experience allowed us to fully see God's hand in our lives. We had been believers for our entire lives, but until that point, we had never truly and fully needed Him. Going through this horrible trial allowed us to learn to completely trust Him and to witness His powerful Grace in our lives. We were still in the middle of the "ocean," but we knew that whatever happened, He would be there for us. God is great, and He will never abandon us or let us fail. He has a greater plan for our lives than we could ever imagine, and I began to trust that no matter what happens, everything is going to be alright. I'm still not happy I got cancer, but I am filled with joy, knowing that whatever happens in my life going forward, my God will be there next me.

CHAPTER FOUR

our miracle baby.

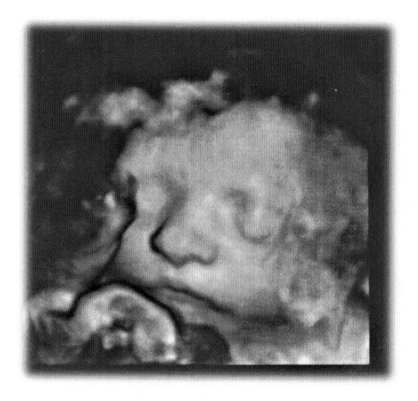

"He shall feed his flock like a shepherd: he shall gather the lambs with his arm, and carry them next to his bosom; and shall gently lead those that are with young."

-Isaiah 40:11 KJV

On New Year's Eve 2014, Mike and I were sitting in an Arby's parking lot in Utah, sipping on chocolate milkshakes and talking about the possibility of having another baby. Our daughter Zoey was turning two the next morning, and we had debated whether we wanted to have our kids closer or further apart. We hadn't felt quite ready for another baby because Zoey had been such a joy to have in our lives. However, on that night, we decided that we were finally ready to grow our family. We were beyond excited.

The next eight months were extremely hard for us as we got negative test after negative test. Any couple trying to get pregnant understands the emotional roller coaster of each cycle; the absolute hope and optimism, followed by disappointment and sadness. It only took me a month to get pregnant with Zoey, and I was very frustrated that it took longer this time around.

But the day finally came! Mike's mom and stepfather were in town visiting, and while they were here, we finally saw those two pink lines. When I told Mike the news, we hugged each other so tight, tears of joy filling our eyes. We were finally going to have another baby! We both secretly hoped for a boy, and at twenty weeks, we found out that our wish was coming true!

We already felt that our baby was a miracle, but we were about to find out how miraculous he truly was. After receiving the good results from my MRI and bone marrow biopsy, we met with my cardiologist. With wonder and excitement, he explained how my baby had saved my life. The tumor had completely blocked off my superior vena cava (one of the two main blood vessels to the heart), and under normal conditions, I would have died due to a lack of circulation. However, because I was pregnant the blood was rerouted through my placenta and the other vessels produced to support my extra blood volume due to pregnancy. The smile on his face beamed with excitement and awe. He said he wished that he could do a CT scan on me every single day just to watch what would happen as the tumor shrank. His excitement was contagious and filled us with so much hope and amazement. Later, my oncologist and obstetrician, as well as many other doctors, confirmed that *my baby saved my life.*

Mike and I were blown away. My doctors believed the cancer had only been growing for about four months, and I was seven months along in my pregnancy. If I had gotten pregnant when I wanted to in January of the previous year, I would be gone right now. In an instant, everything made sense to us. All those months of heartache and disappointment as we tried to get pregnant had a purpose now. I've always believed in miracles but to be a part of one was incredible. It was almost impossible to comprehend that such a tiny little person growing inside me was saving my life, that we were both working together to support each other simultaneously. Mike and I both wept tears of joy as I held my belly and felt Tug move inside of me.

Later that day, Mike surprised me with a beautiful Willow Tree figurine of a little boy holding a sign that said "Hope" and a stuffed animal dinosaur for our son. I again cried tears of joy as we talked about how it felt to be a part of this miracle. Later that day, I had a 3D ultrasound of Tug, and we laughed when we saw his cute little face-he looked just like his big sister.

We couldn't help telling the story to every new nurse that came into our room, and most of them ended up crying with us. Tug was the silver lining to this cancer story—the miracle baby who saved his mama's life. It's a story we'll never be able to stop telling for the rest of our lives.

In just a few short days, we had experienced more grief

and more joy than we ever had in our whole lives. Because of these three days alone, I will never doubt what God can do and will always believe that He is a God of miracles. I'm so grateful for God's perfect love, and I am so grateful for my little boy. I can't wait to tell him his role in this story as he grows up—about how he saved his mama and how God made it possible.

CHAPTER FIVE

our beautiful girl.

"Do all these things; but most important, love each other. Love is what holds you all together in perfect unity."

-Colossians 3:14 ICB

The first couple days in the hospital were the worst. Mike and I were in crisis mode, trying to survive minute by minute, and our family and friends were doing what they could to help support us.

Even though we felt as if we were in the middle of a hurricane, whenever Mike's mom would bring Zoey to visit, we tried to cheer up for her. Each time Zoey arrived she sanitized her hands outside the room, I would hear her say "Washy, Washy," and then she'd run into my room with a huge smile on her face, and I couldn't help but smile back. Although I knew she was happy to see me, I could tell she was scared because she didn't really want to sit with me or touch me. I think that her little heart knew somehow that I was different, and it scared her. It broke my heart because all I wanted to do was hold her.

Despite things being completely different, Mike and I tried to make things as "normal" as possible. While I stayed in the ICU, Mike took Zoey on daddy/daughter dates to the hospital cafeteria. They had dinner together, played in the kids' area, and roamed the halls. On days she was being tended at home, Mike would take off to go spend time with her. He told me he would take naps with her and try to make her feel as if nothing had changed.

One night after Zoey had come to visit, Mike walked her and his mom out to the car. It was always hard for me to say goodbye, but I know it was just as hard for Mike. After he came back, I noticed that he had tears in his eyes. When I asked him what was wrong, he said that Zoey was really upset and told him as she wept, "Daddy come home." He said he broke down crying as he stroked her face in the car seat as she fell asleep. He said it felt like our family was being ripped apart.

A couple of days later my cardiologist suggested I put on some regular clothes before Zoey arrived so I looked more normal. My nurse cleaned up the room and removed some of the unused medical equipment. When Zoey arrived, she ran right over to me with a huge smile and said, "Mama! You all better now?!" I smiled back at her, wishing I could tell her honestly that I was. Despite how sad I felt, it gave me comfort that she felt better being around me.

Later that day, Zoey and I ate popsicles together and spent time drawing pictures of kittens and puppies. Suddenly, Zoey started drawing tears on all the animals I had drawn, and when I asked her about it, she said that they were sad. I knew instantly that this was my precious girl's way of expressing herself, and it made me feel so blue. Even though she didn't understand all that was occurring, she could feel that things were not right.

Later that day, she was snuggling with me, and as I held her she wept. I had never heard her cry that way before. It was a cry of sadness, of sorrow. My heart broke as I held her while she sobbed, and I cried right along with her. It was incredibly hard for me to see my baby hurting. Her whole world had been turned upside down and all I could do was hold her.

I expected many hard days in the future. However, I wanted to believe that getting through that first week was the hardest, and I prayed my beautiful girl would never feel that sad again.

Even though we had some difficult moments that week, there were some great ones too. One time, Zoey rode on the bed with me on my way to get an x-ray, she thought it was the greatest thing ever. She giggled as the orderly pushed us down the hallway and held my hand the entire time. Other great moments included taking naps with her in my hospital bed, watching her sleep, sharing delicious hospital chocolate pudding, and giving her presents that Mike picked out for me to give her.

Looking back, I think one of the most important things we did was making a promise that we would not let cancer ruin our family and that we would try to live each day to the fullest, enjoying our time together. I told Mike that no matter what happened that I didn't want these to be the worst days of our lives, and for the most part, they weren't.

When we made that promise, we knew we were still only at the beginning of our journey, but we were confident that we could do it. We knew that we were still the same family as before, and that we would be stronger when we made it through.

The morning after I was discharged from the hospital, Zoey crawled into my side of the bed. She climbed under the covers, grabbed my hand, and put it on her cheek. In her sweet little voice, she said, "I love you, Mama. I happy you home." My heart melted. Mike wrapped his arms around me, Zoey snuggled in closer, and little Tug moved inside my belly. No thoughts of cancer, of treatments, or what obstacles lay ahead of us. Just the four of us, in our own home, being a family, feeling so incredibly loved and happy. It was a moment I could stay in forever.

CHAPTER SIX

losing my hair.

"Therefore, we do not lose heart. Though outwardly we are wasting away, yet inwardly we are being renewed day by day."

-2 Corinthians 4:16 NIV

When my doctors told me I would lose my hair from chemo, it didn't really bother me. In crisis mode, desperate to get rid of the tumor, my hair was simply the last thing I cared about, and I was willing to exchange it for my life without a second thought.

However, when I got out of the hospital after my initial diagnosis, I went with my stepmom to get a haircut to donate my beautiful, curly brown hair to Locks of Love, and the emotional weight of losing my hair set in. Seeing the hair lie on the floor all around me was traumatic and made this whole cancer thing more of a reality. I walked out of the hair salon with my ponytail in hand and broke into tears. Not because I didn't love my pixie cut or even because I was going bald, but because it was a reminder to me that everything had changed, and it hurt. My stepmom pulled me into a hug, let me cry on her shoulder, and listened to me vent about how frustrated I was that this was happening to me and how I wished things could go back to normal. She held me as I let out all my bottled- up emotions, and even though it hurt, it felt so good to cry. As the week went on, my new pixie cut grew on me.

Mike took me to get some cute headbands, and I had

fun rocking my new hairstyle. However, the pixie was short lived. One morning I woke up and my pillow was covered in hair. When I took a shower, lumps began falling out, and I knew it was time. Later that night, after Zoey was asleep, and we finally had a moment to ourselves, my loving husband shaved my head. We went into our bathroom, he pulled out the clippers, gave me a giant hug, and asked me if I was ready. I looked up at him with tears in my eyes, laughed, and said no—but yes, I was ready.

As my brown hair fell to the floor, and I watched as my appearance changed instantly, I was sad that I had cancer but so incredibly grateful that I had Mike by my side. It was one of the most special, loving, and tender moments we'd had so far in our ten years together. Never in our lifetime would I have thought this was something we would go through, and yet here we were, living out the "in sickness" part of our vows, and it was beautiful.

After he was done, I looked in the mirror and I felt devastated. I started crying, feeling insecure and like I was in someone else's body. As I cried, Mike pulled me into a hug, kissed my bare head, looked me in the eyes, and told me I was beautiful. I've heard him say it thousands of times, but this time was completely new and different than ever before. I knew he meant it with every ounce of his soul because the look in his eyes told me he was telling the truth. In that moment, he made me feel like the most beautiful girl in the world. I wept again as he held me, but this time because I felt so perfectly loved.

That night I wore a beanie hat to bed, so Zoey wouldn't be caught off guard if she saw me before I woke up. I worried about how she would react to seeing me without my hair, that it would harm our relationship. I worried she would see me differently and it would create a distance between us.

When morning came she ran over to my side of the bed and after our good morning snuggles, I took my hat off and showed her my new look. In her cute, soft, inquisitive three-year-old voice, she said, "Oh! Mama! Your hair is all gone!" I told her, "Yes, mama's hair is all gone. Daddy helped me cut it off." She smiled at me, and just said, "Oh! Okay! Mama, you get me milk?" I laughed with delight because my baby still saw me as her mama, and it was exactly what I needed.

Later that day when Mike got home from work, Zoey told him all about my hair being gone and wanted to show him. It was just an event from her day and something different rather than anything traumatic. I was incredibly relieved and grateful that my baldness didn't change anything between the two people I loved the most.

I really loved my natural hair—it was such a huge part of my identity. I loved how thick yet soft it was. I loved that I could curl it or straighten it, and in the summertime, it would lighten up in the sun. I knew I would miss it, but I could come to terms that it may be gone permanently.

Everyone told me I looked great bald because I had "such a nice round head." But the problem was that I still felt awkward looking at myself in the mirror. It was as if a stranger was peering back at me and it made me uncomfortable. I wasn't ready to wear wigs yet, so I started wearing scarves and loved them. They gave variety to my look and made me feel more confident.

Losing my hair was hard. It made me feel insecure and ugly. But it was just hair, and I knew I had bigger problems to worry about. I remembered the ICU's social worker's advice—I had to take things one day at a time and not be concerned about my outer appearance. I needed to focus on the good—like the fact that I was married to a man who truly loved me for who I was and not how I appeared, who made me feel beautiful whether I had hair or not. I had to focus on my daughter and be content knowing that she still saw me as her mama, and that our relationship had not changed. Even though I lost my hair, the people I loved most still thought I was beautiful. My outer appearance had changed, but inside I was still the same. I saw that my family loved me with true, unconditional, perfect love—and that was worth more than any strand of hair could ever be.

CHAPTER SEVEN

weeks off.

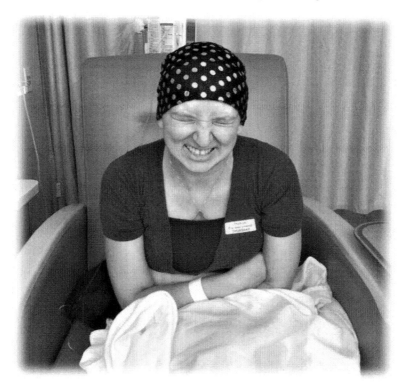

"May the Lord bless you and keep you. May the Lord show you his kindness. May he have mercy on you. May the Lord watch over you and give you peace."

-Numbers 6: 24-26 ICB

After each round of chemo, I was given two weeks off. Each round took at least five days of inpatient chemo, followed by two weeks of outpatient recovery; it was a three-week long roller-coaster. I would start the first week feeling good, before rapidly going downhill the second, slowly climbing back up to the third, and just as I felt well again, it started all over. Calling them "weeks off" was a joke—fighting cancer was a full-time job and breaks were not allowed.

To get treatment, I had to get a PICC Line (Peripheral Inserted Central Catheter) placed. Since chemo drugs can be very damaging to smaller blood vessels, they need to be injected into larger ones deeper inside the body. Due to the blocked veins in my chest, where they would normally insert the line, they instead had mine placed in my femoral artery in my upper thigh. My first chemotherapy treatment was administered in the ICU, and the line they had placed was only meant to be temporary. To go forward with the remaining five rounds, I needed to have a new line placed.

After fasting all night, I was prepped for the PICC Line placement procedure. The nurses placed an IV in the pit of my elbow and gave me drugs to help sedate me. Because I was pregnant, they couldn't give me a lot of the sedative, which meant that I was still very aware of the pain and what was occurring. They first tried to place one in my chest, using an X-ray machine to guide the catheter. As they reached the middle of my neck, it stopped going forward, and I could feel the eerie, uncomfortable sensation of wires poking around inside me. It freaked me out, causing me to panic, and I ended up fainting on the table. I woke up surrounded by panicked doctors and nurses reviving me, a cold, wet towel on my forehead. It scared me that I had lost consciousness, and when I came-to I again panicked.

The doctor explained that after discovering that the PICC line could not be inserted in my chest, due to the damage done by the lymphoma tumor, he would be inserting it in my femoral artery.

Normally, this procedure would be over within thirty minutes, but I had been in there for over two hours. They finally got a PICC line placed in my upper thigh and took me to the recovery room.

Having a central catheter anywhere, and especially in the lower half of the body, can increase the risk of infection in the bloodstream. Each week the dressing that covered the catheter site was cleaned and changed. Anytime I was given anything through my line it had to be sanitized properly to avoid germs entering. Showering was a real chore since the line could not get wet. It took over twenty minutes for me to cover it up. First, I would place layers of paper towels over the bandage, then cover it with a plastic film. Next, I would tape around all the edges with two different types of tape, wrapping all the way around my thigh. I couldn't take a bath, which would have been easier because I was always so tired and weak. Despite how careful I was to cover everything, water often got inside. The recommendation was to bathe every day, and since that was so difficult, they gave me sanitizing wipes to sponge bathe instead. They smelled of chemicals, and made my skin feel itchy and dry.

Almost every day during my off weeks, I had appointments with my oncologist. When I first met her, I could tell she was a strong woman. She was very stoic and kept her distance from me. As we got to know each other, she really opened up, and I saw how incredibly caring and kindhearted she was. I felt that the combination of strength and softness made her an exceptional doctor. As an oncologist, she had watched too many people experience the devastating effects of cancer, and yet remains optimistic and capable of offering comfort and hope. I always appreciated how genuine she was, and how straight she always was with me. I felt confident with her decisions, trusting that she was a person of true integrity. Not once did I feel the need to get second opinions—I trusted her completely. She worked so hard to not only treat my illness but also to improve my mental state. I loved that she always played and interacted with my kids, that she treated Mike as a friend, and that she truly listened to me and my concerns with compassion.

For days after chemo, my oncologist ordered many blood tests to observe my health status. My PICC line was such a blessing because instead of constantly getting poked in my arms to have blood drawn, they could pull it straight from my line. Since it was high on my thigh, jeans were out of the question, and my wardrobe consisted of leggings, gym shorts, and maxi skirts. The skirts were my favorite because I wouldn't have to drop my drawers to get my blood drawn, I could just hike my skirt up enough to access the line. It made me feel more modest and less exposed.

Lymphoma is a form of blood cancer, and the type of

chemotherapy treatment given targets and kills not only cancerous but also healthy blood cells, making the immune system vulnerable, heightening the risk of dangerous infections. My white blood count declined quickly in the first few days, but my red blood count dropped slowly over a couple of weeks. Part of my daily visits to my oncologist were to monitor my blood cell count. If my white blood count was too low, I was required to wear a mask, watch for fevers, report instantly if my temperature went up, and visit the emergency room where they would administer high doses of antibiotics, antivirals, and antifungal medications. If my red blood count was too low, I would start feeling anemic, with symptoms of major fatigue, insomnia, and a racing heart. This happened a couple of times, and I was sent to the infusion center in the hospital for a blood transfusion that would take four hours to receive.

During those long hours, I would stare at the bag of blood, imagining the person who had given me this precious gift. I would feel gratitude for them, knowing that they had sacrificed their time, endured the pain of a needle in their vein, and given their own precious blood to help a stranger like me.

As the blood dripped into my body, I began to feel more energetic, less anxious, my heartbeat slowing and my body warming. I thought it was odd that I loved getting blood. I joked that I felt like a vampire because the transfusions made me feel a lot better and quickly, too!

In addition to daily lab draws, I was required to give myself GSF (Growth Stimulating Factor) shots in my abdomen to prepare my body for when my blood cells would be very low. To treat the blood clots in my jugular veins, my oncologist put me on twice-daily blood-thinning shots. I had to give myself injections every single morning and night. For someone who used to be terrified of shots, I overcame my fear and became very skilled at stabbing myself. Though I got over my fear, it was still painful, and the medicine made me bruise extremely easy. My body, and especially my stomach, looked as if I had been beaten with a baseball bat. Injectable blood thinners are easier than oral medication to maintain while going through chemo, which meant I would spend the next year dealing with these awful shots before I was finally switched to a pill.

In addition to the many oncology appointments, I also saw my cardiologist, and obstetrics doctor weekly. My cardiologist was constantly checking for reoccurrence of pericardial effusions and other heart conditions that chemo can cause. For a couple months after my first pericardial effusion, I panicked every time I felt like my heart rate was too high, afraid that my heart sac was filling with more fluid and that I would once again need to undergo the painful heart tap procedure. To monitor me, my cardiologist ordered many echo-cardiograms (an ultrasound procedure to view the heart). I had twenty-nine of them done in 2015 and became the Evergreen Hospital record holder for most heart-echoes received in one year!

Visits with my cardiologist always made me worry less—he was so encouraging and hopeful, always reassuring me that he would do all he could to keep my heart healthy. He was very protective over me and worked in harmony with the other doctors on my team. I will always be grateful for how much he cared and how hard he worked to keep me alive.

My obstetrician was a high-risk pregnancy physician. I had an ultrasound at each weekly visit and was able to see my sweet baby. Seeing that Tug was doing so well was comforting. I also had NSTs (non-stress tests) to check on Tug. For thirty minutes, with straps and monitors wrapped tightly around my pregnant belly, I listened to his heart beat. My obstetrician and the nurses were always thrilled with his results, despite the immense amount of stress he was going through. I was so proud of him, amazed that such a small, unborn human could be so strong!

When I was home, I tried budgeting my energy. There was so much I wanted to do, but I would fatigue quickly if I pushed myself too hard. I was forced to take things slower, shorten my to-do list, schedule time to relax. Self-care was of ultimate importance.

On days I felt well enough, we tried to get out with the kids. Since I was instructed to stay away from crowds and tight spaces with other people to prevent infections, we spent time outdoors, soaking in the sunshine at the beach, watching the kids play in the forest, resting on a bench as Zoey made new friends on playgrounds, and taking walks around our community. We shopped at odd hours when stores were empty and went for a lot of drives. I tried to help as much as I could with daily chores and managing our household, but truthfully Mike and our family were the ones doing most of the work. I enjoyed the many delicious home-cooked meals that family and friends brought over— each meal tasting a million times better than the nasty hospital food I choked down while I was an inpatient. I read a lot, took naps with my babies, and after their bedtimes, snuggled up with Mike on the couch and watched shows, usually falling asleep in his arms.

Although my "weeks off" were still a ton of work, it was always better being home, sleeping in my own cozy bed, eating my own food, and surrounded by the most precious people in my life. There is no place on earth I'd rather be, then or now. For as they say, home is where the heart is.

CHAPTER EIGHT

God is good.

"Surely your goodness and love will follow me all the days of my life, and I will dwell in the house of the LORD forever."

-Psalms 23: 6 KJV

Exactly one week before I went into the ER, I was feeling down, so Mike surprised me by taking me to Alki Beach in Seattle to watch the sunset over Puget Sound. It was a beautiful day. The temperature was a nice sixty degrees with clear skies (rare for Seattle winters), so we set out and found a spot on the beach where we could soak in the beauty. I wasn't feeling well; it was hard for me to walk without getting tired and I had a horrible cough. But I found a log to sit on, and I watched as my two loves walked the beach looking for seashells. The fresh sea breeze filled my hurting lungs, soothing them, and I watched as seagulls flew overhead. About three hundred yards from where I sat, a couple was taking engagement photos with beautiful Mount Rainier in the background. I watched as the sun fell towards the horizon, and the colors changed from blue to pinks and oranges, with silhouetted sailboats floating on the calm grey water. I have seen many sunsets on many beautiful beaches, but this sunset felt like it was meant just for me. In that moment, I felt so overwhelmed with gratitude and joy, thinking about how good God had been to me, and how I was so incredibly blessed to live in such a beautiful place, close to the sea, where I could witness such beauty. I thought about how blessed I was to have a husband that after ten years I was still madly in love with, a daughter that filled my heart with joy, and a son growing inside me, who in just a couple of short months I would get to meet. My life felt so perfect and complete in that moment, and I felt absolute joy. That night, I posted a picture of the scene on Instagram with the caption, "What a beautiful life I have. God is good."

In the weeks following that evening as we faced so many changes, I would often wish we could rewind time and just enjoy the peace and safety of that moment. Immediately after my diagnosis, it felt like we were caught up in a false reality. I just couldn't believe that this was really happening, and I wished I could wake up from this nightmare and go back to the life I had before.

With God's grace, we were handling the whole situation very well. Most days, and most moments we were just the same Mike and Kaylie we were before cancer happened. God truly lifted us up, and I am still amazed at the strength He gave us. But even though we felt Jesus lifting us, there were still moments when reality would come crashing in, and it was too much to handle.

During my many hospital stays, I handled the days fairly well, as I spent time with friends and family. Nights though were much more difficult. When the nurses were done taking care of me and visitors left, I was left alone in the hospital room with my thoughts, unable to block my fears from breaking down the walls I had built during the day.

Even though my prognosis was very optimistic, baby Tug was doing well, and I was much healthier than the day I walked into the ER, there were still so many unknowns, like going through the C-section with my heart in poor condition and my veins still closed off. That terrified me. I feared that I wouldn't make it through the surgery and that my family would be left here on earth without me. I did not fear death, because of my faith in Heaven where I would be with Jesus—but I did not want to leave my beautiful life yet. I felt like there was so much I still wanted to do. I worried about my family, especially Mike. The whole experience of cancer made me think about how fragile life really was, and it scared me that I had no control over what could happen.

One night I was having an especially hard time, and when Mike FaceTimed me to say goodnight, I was in tears. I wept, sharing all these fears with him, and he cried with me. We talked about all our worries, prayed together, and said our goodnights. It was a long night, and I cried myself to sleep.

The next morning, I was scheduled to have a heart-echo done, and the tech that came in was so sweet. I had met her before, but that morning she shared with me the tremendous trial she had been through, and how she had been praying for me. We talked about how even though our trials weren't the same, we had the shared experience of not having control over our lives and truly needing God to lift us up. We both had felt absolute vulnerability, brokenness, and fear. But we also talked about how God had been and still is there for us through it all. After talking and crying together, we realized we went to the same church! In that moment, I knew that God had sent me an angel to help me through this experience, and it brought me increased strength in my moment of weakness. I was so grateful to meet a new friend and for her encouragement. Her being there for me, that day, after having one of the worst nights, was exactly what I needed and reminded me that God never leaves us alone.

This was just one experience where the right person was there at the right time. I met the most incredible people because of my illness, like the night nurse in the ICU who had the same cancer as me, and who came to visit me every time I was in the hospital. He encouraged me and offered me so much hope. Another nurse, who just finished going through chemo, was Christian and prayed with me when I was feeling down. Countless people encouraged me along the way. Just when I would start to feel alone, someone would show up for a visit, a card would arrive in the mail, or I'd receive an encouraging text message—all reminders that I was never alone.

Cancer changed everything. Our lives got flipped upside down. Throughout it all, Mike and I tried our hardest to be grateful for each moment and for the blessings in our lives. There was always the fear that I might not make it out of this, but from that fear we learned that when we started to doubt, we had to choose faith instead. Because the truth is, no one is guaranteed more than today. A car accident, natural disaster, or any number of things could take away our lives in a moment. We don't know how much time we have here on earth, and while that is scary, it is also a reason to fully live in each moment and appreciate the beautiful people we have in our lives. We can't worry about the future we must live for today.

I don't like focusing on the unknowns because the fear cripples me and robs me of joy. Each day, during my with cancer and ever since, I make a conscious effort to focus on all the good things in my life and choose to trust that no matter what happens, God loves and cares about me and everyone who has ever lived. I don't always succeed at accomplishing this goal, but I am trying with all my heart to do so. When things become too much to bear, I hand my concerns and worries over to God, and He helps me carry the burden. I have so many reasons to still smile and find joy in my life. I can't rewind time, go back to that sunset on Alki beach, and erase all that has happened. But I can still caption my days with the same phrase as my Instagram post— "What a beautiful life I have. God is good!"

CHAPTER NINE

weak and strong.

"That is why, for Christ's sake, I delight in weaknesses, in insults, in hardships, in persecutions, in difficulties. For when I am weak, then I am strong."

-2 Corinthians 12:10 NIV

During my pregnancy in the middle of my treatment, I came to understand the words of Paul—that when I am weak then I am strong. I was about thirty weeks pregnant when I recorded my feelings in my journal:

My body is skinny, bruised, and weak. I look down at my arms and legs, and they lack any muscle definition. I have purple and black bruises all over. A bandage covers the catheter tubes coming out of my thigh, which are connected to the red-tinted chemo being pumped into my veins. My mouth is dry, covered in canker sores; heartburn nags at my throat, and everything tastes bland. The nerves in my fingers tingle, and my back and ribs ache from the growing uterus pushing from underneath. My face is pale, and my eyes look tired and slightly sunken in. I look in the mirror and see a bald stranger with only a couple patches of hair leftover. I've never felt more exhausted and weak in my entire life. It's hard for me to do anything except rest.

I may feel and look broken, but I'm also in absolute awe at the incredible things this body is accomplishing. Not only is my body killing cancer, it is also creating a human being!

New life grows inside me; a baby boy who depends on me completely to provide him with strength and nourishment. I'm amazed that despite how sick I was before I started treatment (and even now), my body was still able to provide the proper nutrients and strength this baby boy needed to grow, and he has held on and thrived. I feel him move, his little feet pushing out so hard into my side that I can see the exact size and shape of his sweet baby feet. I can tell when he's sleeping, when he's wide awake, and even when he has the hiccups!

I hold my belly, picturing the moment when I get to embrace him in my arms and kiss his sweet baby cheeks. I'm anxious to see what he looks like. Whether, like his big sister, he has my smile and gapped front teeth and his daddy's eyes and crooked big toe. Whether he'll come out bald and match me, or if he has hair that was protected by my placenta.

I have been dreaming about the moment Zoey first sees and holds him; I picture the smile and wonder in her eyes as she meets her lifetime friend for the first time. If she's anything like me, she'll instantly become his second mom and spend her life nurturing and bossing him around like I did my siblings. She will worry about him, want to protect him, and love him unconditionally as they experience life together.

I anticipate with excitement the happy tears that will roll

down our faces as Mike and I meet this miracle boy, and the pure joy we will feel as our infant son falls asleep on our chests and we smell and feel his soft baby skin, as we hold him and ponder the beautiful creation he is, like we all are.

Every baby is a miracle; a beautiful gift from God. We are perfectly designed and created. I feel so incredibly blessed to be a woman who is capable of growing new life and bringing a precious soul to this beautiful earth. Life truly is a gift.

CHAPTER TEN
time, unity, goodness.

"How good and pleasant it is when God's people
live together in unity!"

-Psalm 133:1 NIV

The fourth week of my treatment proved to be one of the hardest. I underwent another heart tap to drain the additional fluid in my pericardial sac that had accumulated since the last one. It was supposed to be a straightforward procedure, and I was expected to go home the next day. But it was extremely painful, and as my cardiologist placed the needles into my heart, the pain was unbearable, and I sobbed in gasps on the table. My friend, the heart-echo tech, was there with me and helped comfort me, for which I was grateful. But I could tell by the look on her face that she felt utterly sorry for me because she knew I was in so much pain.

The day after the procedure, my cardiologist and oncologist came into my room and gave Mike and I the bad news. The fluid they had pulled out was a milky white color, indicating it was lymphatic fluid that was draining into my pericardial sac. They told me that there have only been thirty-three other cases where this had happened, and they couldn't take the drain out because my heart would continue to fill up. They were going to transfer me to the University of Washington where there were experts and specialists who would be able to help me better.

For the first time in over eight weeks, I cried in front

of my doctors. Up until that point, I had been strong when I was with them, but I was so sad that they wouldn't be able to take care of me anymore. They explained that they weren't exactly sure what was going to happen, but most likely I would need some type of open chest surgery to fix the problem. They arranged my transfer, and that night Mike and I rode in an ambulance for the very first time to the UW Medical Center.

We were both upset that once again, our plans were being changed and we had no control over the circumstances. Uncertainty is the worst, and we were extremely frightened. However, being at UW Medical Center eventually gave us a much clearer picture of what would happen next, and that helped us feel more secure.

I was placed in the Cardiac ICU and was continuously monitored by nurses, medical students, residents, and doctors. UW Medical Center is a teaching hospital, so I was constantly bombarded by medical students, residents, and attending physician. Each team, (cardiology, oncology, and obstetric) rounded daily, overwhelming me with their many visits, as each provider asked questions about me while I lay in a hospital bed being studied. My case was unique, and I became a popular patient for inquisitive minds.

The cardiology team decided to leave the drain in place, causing excruciating pain, so I was given a lot of narcotics to handle it. Being in pain made me weepy and emotional, and the medications made me groggy and frustrated.

A week after being transferred to UW Medical Center, I was scheduled to have my C-section. It was the day that had made me most nervous and excited since all this had begun. After all this time, I was going to meet my little boy, who had kept me safe and tugged me along the way. We decided to name our son Tug, a name which has great significant to us. To explain why, I need to go back to the beginning of our relationship.

When I was sixteen years old, I was just an innocent, twitter-patted teen, caught up in a high school romance. I had no idea what qualities I truly wanted in a future husband, but I quickly fell in love with this boy that everyone called "Tug." He was so sweet to me, always so attentive, thoughtful, and caring. He made me laugh, and he loved having fun. He would go completely out of his way to do nice things for me, and he treated my family and his so well. I never thought I would be that girl who would marry her high school boyfriend at age nineteen, but it was the best decision I ever made.

In our first ten years as a couple, we had already been through so much together, from buying a house, graduating from college, having our daughter, and moving to Washington. But now we were going through the biggest trial of our lives while simultaneously expecting our second child. Things had turned out very different than I had imagined ten years ago.

When we asked our bishop to marry us almost seven years before, he offered to write vows for us if we didn't want to write our own. We were nervous and shy in front of others, so we had him do the honors. In our vows, he used the acronym T.U.G.

Time

Unity

Goodness

He talked about how you needed these three things to have a good marriage. Nothing else was more important to do or get done than spending time together as a couple and as a family. Time was essential to continually strengthen our relationship. He discussed how we needed to be united, that no matter what happened we would always be on each other's team and always be supportive. And lastly, we needed to have goodness. We needed to speak kind words, have respect, and do good things for one another.

Throughout our marriage and especially during our fight against cancer, we have made these things a priority. We have lived out these wedding vows, and I can truly say it has made all the difference. I could not have gotten through cancer, let alone all the other hard challenges in our marriage without Mike. I am beyond grateful that he has been by my side. He made it a top priority to be with me as much as he could while I was in the hospital and to bring our daughter to see me. It wasn't easy, driving thirty minutes each way, back and forth from home, staying up late, and entertaining a toddler in a hospital, but he made sure that we were together as a family every single day.

We also became more united than ever before. Through all the tears and all the pain, we have drawn closer. Some of the most memorable moments for me during this time were when I was sad or in pain and my sweet husband wrapped me in his arms and just held me. With so much uncertainty and such a large uphill battle ahead of us, our marriage and our friendship have been our solid ground, a safe place to weather the storm.

Lastly, our marriage is founded on goodness. Just like when we first dated, Mike is incredibly sweet and good to me. He is kind, loving, and still makes me laugh, even when times are hard. Even though I was often unable to do anything, he never complained. He treated me with respect and went out of his way to make me comfortable.

The night before Tug's birth, I wrote the following from my hospital bed:

Tomorrow morning, we will meet our son, and Zoey will meet her baby brother. We are naming him Tug after his daddy, and after our wedding vows. Time, Unity, and Goodness—three words that have brought our family closer together over the years, and especially during our enormous trial. The amount of love I feel for this little family of mine is indescribable. I have been truly blessed to be married to such an amazing man and to make beautiful children with him.

We are thankful for our Father in Heaven. Without His guidance and His Grace, we know that we wouldn't be where we are today. The last two months have been scary and hard, but we have come so far, and we are getting closer to the day that I finally get that clean bill of health. It has been very hard for us to endure the pain, stress, and anxiety that this cancer has brought, but with God's Grace, we have been lifted up and have made it through. We know all good things come from Him, and we will never stop thanking Him for allowing us to have this beautiful story to call our own. It's a story of great trial and tribulation, but also a story of great love and hope. Tomorrow morning is the day we have been waiting for: The day we get to meet our little Tug; the day our family grows, and we can see once again the miracle of life.

CHAPTER ELEVEN

tug's birth.

"Before I formed you in the womb I knew
you, before you were born I set you apart;"

-Jeremiah 1:5 NIV

From the moment I was diagnosed, I had been concerned about delivering Tug. With Zoey, I unfortunately had a placental abruption (premature separation of the placenta from the uterine lining), causing me to lose a lot of blood, and putting my baby at great risk. She was delivered via emergency C-section. I knew delivering Tug would be even more difficult due to my health status. In addition to my experience as a patient, I also worked for four years after high school as a Surgical Technologist and taught as a Surgical Tech Instructor at a local college. I knew the name of every instrument and what they were used for. I had helped assist in hysterectomies, which are similar in many ways, and helped surgeons as they cut through layers of skin, muscle, and worked around delicate organs. I was familiar with the smell of burning tissue from the cauterization instrument. I knew that when they made it to the inner layers, they would pull from both sides of the table, using their entire body weight to stretch and tear the muscles apart to gain access to the uterus. It disturbed me that this would be happening to me as I lay strapped to the operating table, awake and aware.

I believe that knowledge is power, and that most of the

time, the more I know, the better. However, being a patient on the table instead of standing next to it made me wish I could forget what I had learned. I would have preferred to have been oblivious to it all, rather than having the feeling of familiarity. It made my anxiety shoot through the roof.

What scared me the most was knowing how stressful it was for my body to undergo such a major procedure. Even for healthy women, delivering a baby is extremely taxing, but with my health status, the stakes were much higher.

The night before, I was unable to sleep, thoughts and worries running through my mind, prayers pouring out of my soul. The next day arrived quickly, and Mike and I FaceTimed Zoey, who was back at home with Mike's mom. We told her that her brother was going to be here soon, and with an adorable, excited grin, she gave me a moment of relief.

After talking with our sweet girl, Mike helped me change into a new hospital gown and socks. Next, he helped me put my scarf over my hairless scalp. I had specifically chosen a red one, in hopes that I would feel more powerful wearing it as I underwent one of the biggest moments of my life. After dressing me up for the event, he sat at the edge of my hospital bed, held me in his arms, and prayed over me, tears rolling down both our faces.

My dad came into the room, hugged me, and told me he was proud of me. I felt tremendously protected by the two most important men in my life, and I thanked them for always being there for me.

The nurse came into the room and pushed my bed to the maternity wing, that was all the way on the other side of the hospital, Mike and my dad walking beside me. When we arrived, they each gave me one more hug, and I was pushed through the two heavy doors, leaving them behind.

I thought I could hold it all together, but once things got underway I knew I wouldn't be able to. My favorite maternity nurse helped me climb onto the operating table, wrapped warm blankets around my shoulders, and gave me a hug. It was then that I began to unravel, sobbing as the fear rushed over me. I was scared but also overwhelmed with all the emotions I was feeling. I felt uncomfortable being in that environment, anxious to get the spinal anesthetic, excited to meet my son, desperate for Mike to be with me, and absolutely grateful that I had carried this baby all the way to thirty-five weeks when no one thought I was going to make it past twenty-six. Every feeling, good and bad, that I'd felt over the last two months came rushing in, and it was impossible not to pour them out. The nurse wiped my tears with my blanket and encouraged me, her eyes locked on mine. I sat with my back hunched, and she held me up as the anesthesiologist poked around my spine, looking for the right spot to access my spinal cord to numb me for the procedure. While he pushed the extra-long needles into my back, I recoiled in pain and wept in her arms. She continued to tell me that I would be okay, my baby would be okay, and that this would all be over soon.

The anesthesiologist got the spinal nerve block in and laid me down on the table. As my lower body started to go numb, they prepped and draped my belly and continued to hook me up to monitors. Finally, they let Mike come in, and as soon as I had his hand in mine I felt instant relief. Having him there to encourage and support me made me feel at ease, and from that point on only positive feelings remained.

The surgery went perfect. I felt no pain as they worked, just eerie tugging and pulling sensations. With Zoey, I didn't feel anything because I had been in labor for eight hours before she was delivered in the operating room. But with Tug, I felt almost everything, and even though it wasn't painful, it was uncomfortable and weird. After what seemed like forever, I felt the doctors push on the top of my belly, and shortly after they announced that Tug was here! The smile on Mike's face and the tears in his eyes made for a moment I'll never forget.

They quickly took Tug over to the NICU team, waiting in the corner with massive amounts of equipment, for a preemie checkup. Mike followed them and helped cut the cord. It took a second for Tug to cry, but when he did, I burst into tears. I looked over at Mike, and with tears streaming down his face, he mouthed the words, "I love you" to me. I said, "I love you" back, and we looked at each other, filled to the brim with joy. After they felt that Tug was stable, they brought him over to me on the operating table and put his cheek up against mine. I had been waiting for that moment since I found out I was pregnant.

Our little boy had made it here safely. The eight weeks after I was diagnosed, plus the months of pregnancy before that, had been hard and scary. The constant anxiety about whether our baby was going to be okay was overwhelming. Each chemo treatment, the fear would build, and our prayers increased.

Finally, Tug arrived, and he was perfect! Despite being a preemie, he had no breathing problems and weighed six pounds! His only issue was that he wasn't eating enough to make the doctors happy. He had more hair than me, and to see his dark, silky locks was proof to me that the chemo had had little effect on him. Lying on that operating table, I gave a silent prayer of gratitude to Heavenly Father, thanking Him for protecting me and Tug so that we could make it to this beautiful day.

After the procedure, Mike went with Tug, and my dad met me in recovery. He looked as relieved as I was, and he gave me a huge hug. Shortly after, I was in excruciating pain, because there had been a mix up about what medications I should be receiving. For about forty-five minutes, my pain was excruciating, and I sobbed violently. As my dad held my hand, I could see in his eyes how helpless he felt watching me suffer. They finally got my pain under control and brought my newborn baby into the room to see me.

As I held him, I wept again, but this time out of pure happiness. I looked at Tug's perfect little face and thanked him for saving me and being with me during this crazy cancer journey. We had been through a lot together, and my heart felt so full of love for my tiny human. A couple minutes later, they brought Zoey into the room. She ran over to my bed, a huge smile on her face, and Mike lifted her up to see. We introduced her to her baby brother, and in her cute toddler voice, she giggled and said, "He has a funny face!" It was so adorable, and everyone in the room laughed with delight. My ten-year-old sister also came over to see Tug, and she started crying as well. I asked her why and she said, "He's just so beautiful!"

Because I was in the ICU and Tug was in the NICU, it was hard for us to be together, and so I only saw him for about two hours a day for the first week of his life. It was hard for me to be separated from him, and to simultaneously be going through more painful procedures and tests to fix my pericardial effusion. So, the moments I did see him, I truly savored. Those two hours were what carried me through the rest of the day.

Seeing Zoey become a big sister was exactly as I had imagined. She was absolutely fascinated by the tiny baby, and I loved seeing her nurturing side come out. When he cried, she'd go over to him and say, "It's okay, baby, it'll be okay." She'd give him kisses on the cheeks and try to play hide-and-seek with him. She took her baby doll that my parents had given her everywhere and copied Mike when he was holding Tug. I loved seeing my daydreams of her as a sister come true.

Mike is an incredible dad. Although I knew it the moment he held Zoey for the first time, he has proven it time and time again. I was blown away at how strong he had been through all of this. Not only did he support me, but he held our family together. He helped Zoey cope with me being gone and made sure she felt as normal as possible. We had a lot of help from family, and we couldn't have done it without them. But Mike was the captain of our team, who kept us going. Nothing makes me love him more than seeing him be a daddy to his two babies.

Although Tug's delivery was incredible, my doctors still needed to figure out why my lymphatic system was leaking into my heart and determine a way to stop it. I still had that painful drain in my heart, and every day the cardiology residents would drain and rinse it. It was painful as they shot the saline solution through the drain and pulled it back out. They restricted my diet to only extremely low-fat foods and talked of major open chest surgeries. Before surgery, they wanted to determine where it was leaking, so on two days after Tug's delivery, they sent me to have a lymphatic study done to see how the lymphatic fluid was leaking into my heart. The test required that they inject radioactive dye between my toes, and every couple of hours they took me back to the imaging room to be scanned to see how the lymphatic fluid was flowing through my lymph vessels.

While we were waiting for the test results, my temperature and heart rate skyrocketed. This was an indication of an infection, caused by the drain in my heart. Suddenly, they were rushing me to the procedure room to remove the drain and replace it. My blood pressure was too low, so they couldn't sedate me very well, and I felt everything. It was excruciating. As I sobbed, I felt as if no one was hearing me. They were all focused on the procedure, and I felt like I was being tortured.

After it was over, my dad and Mike were waiting for me outside the room, each one grabbing my hand with concerned looks on their faces. We got stuck in the elevator for a minute, causing us all to panic. I was convinced my dad and Mike were ready to break walls down, scared out of their minds for me.

During the procedure, they took a sample of the fluid and the lab results showed that I had a staph infection in my heart! They started me on IV penicillin and told me that I would be on it twenty-four hours a day for an entire month. The staph infection in my heart was serious and required the highest dose of penicillin available. I would be going home with the supplies to wear a continuous pump and change the IV medication at home.

I was trying so hard to keep things together, but I looked over at my dad and told him I didn't know how I was ever going to get through this. He held my hand, trying to smile, and told me he knew I would. Meanwhile, Mike went to the waiting room where his mom was watching my sister and Zoey, and he broke down in front of her.

The week of Tug's birth was one of the hardest I'd faced—but it was also one of the most incredible. I finally got to meet my miracle baby, my son and my buddy who had been through so much with me. I got to see my beautiful firstborn become a big sister and watch her tender, nurturing heart fall in love with her new partner-in-crime. I felt the extraordinary love my dad had for me, his first-born child. I also felt more loved by Mike than ever before, and I fell even deeper in love with him as I watched him take care of all of us.

Despite all the challenges we went through, I felt incredibly blessed. I had a beautiful, loving family, and I thank God every single day that he made it possible for our family to grow and become more complete with the addition of our perfect little baby, Tug.

A few days after they replaced my heart drain, and the lymphatic tests were complete, the lymphatic fluid miraculously stopped leaking. They think that it was caused by the extra fluid and pressure from the pregnancy, and after Tug was delivered my body could reestablish its equilibrium. We were beyond relieved knowing that there would be no major chest surgeries in my future. The drain stopped filling, and the cardiologists decided it was time to remove it. The attending cardiologist told me to hum very loud, as he pulled the drain. I did, and as he pulled, I felt an indescribable creepy feeling inside my chest.

Once they removed the drain, they wanted me to spend one more day in the ICU for supervision. It was the night before Easter and I knew that Mike's mom would be coming in the morning with Zoey. I asked Mike to bring me Easter stuff that the "bunny" could leave for her.

The next morning, I got up early and wobbled around

the ICU room, holding onto my IV stand, hiding eggs in the hospital room. I was slow, and it hurt, but I was so excited to do something for my girl. When she arrived, a smile lit up her entire face. It was what I had desperately needed and wanted, and it felt amazing!

Later that day they moved me to another wing of the hospital that was more private. For several days after Tug's birth, I was in the ICU and he was in the NICU, which meant constant supervision from nurses. Once I was moved, and he was discharged from the NICU, I finally got to snuggle my baby boy alone. For hours, I held him in my arms, staring at his beautiful face, watching him sleep, feeding him, enjoying his soft, silky skin against mine, and feeling overwhelmed with gratitude. This little boy saved my life, and it took a lot to get him here safely. At six pounds and only a week old, he'd already been through three rounds of chemotherapy and so many other traumatic things. Part of me felt sad that he was out because all along I had him with me, but I was more grateful that he didn't have to go through any more. Instead of being safe in my belly, he was now safely in my arms, and it felt incredible.

CHAPTER TWELVE

changing expectations.

"Take delight in the LORD, and he will give you the desires of your heart."

-Psalm 37:4 NIV

Once Tug and I could be in the same room, I felt relieved to finally have our entire family together. After all the struggles we'd been through, it felt wonderful to have a moment where we sort of felt normal again. We spent Easter relaxing, watching movies, coloring with Zoey, cuddling our newborn, and napping without being constantly interrupted by medical staff. But later that night as Mike left, holding Tug's car seat on one arm, and Zoey's hand with the other, my heart broke. My family was going home without me, and I cried all night long. It was one of the saddest nights of my life.

When I imagined Tug's birth and what it would be like to take him home for the first time, I had beautiful, normal expectations. I pictured bringing him into his room, changing him into his new pajamas, getting Zoey ready for bed, and rocking them both in our rocking chair by the fire. I imagined lying on our bed, with our two babies sleeping in between us, and watching them while Mike and I talked about how perfect their little faces were. I never imagined that I would have to say goodbye to them, night after night, my heart leaving with them. I cried every night, and the only relief came when I would receive pain meds, slipping into sleep. I hated that I was separated from my babies.

Three months after my diagnosis, I had already spent seven weeks in the hospital. So much time away from home, being poked and prodded, tested and analyzed. It's impossible to sleep in a hospital when you're constantly being interrupted with nurses checking vital signs, housekeepers cleaning, nasty hospital food being delivered three times a day, and doctors rounding. I was thoroughly exhausted, but the hardest part for our family was the separation. Even though Mike and our other caretakers made it a top priority to come visit me each day, it still was not the same. In the hospital it was hard to have uninterrupted time together, to snuggle, laugh, play, bond, and be ourselves.

We had to become extremely flexible, throw out the expectations of what we thought life would be like, and accept the reality of what truly was. We had to take things one day at a time, sometimes even one hour at a time. It was far from easy, and each time I saw Mike I could see the pure exhaustion in his eyes from holding us together. But somehow during all this chaos, we managed to make a "new normal."

Even though things were far from what I wanted for our family, there were still some incredible and memorable moments spent in the hospital together. I saw her face light up every single time she walked into my room, and watched the joy spread across it as she ran over to give me a hug. I took countless naps with my Zoey, snuggling her and watching her breathe with her soft curls resting on my chest. It was really hard on me because out of all my relationships, I felt like my illness took the greatest toll on my relationship with my daughter. I felt like she no longer saw me as her caretaker, but rather as a friend. As a three-year-old, her number one way to connect with people was by playing, and I was simply not able to do that. My body was weak, I was tired and fragile, and she knew. During one of my treatments, she had a bad cold and needed to be home. One of our trusted friends took great care of her; however, as a mother it broke me to pieces knowing I wasn't the one holding and comforting her.

Deep down, I knew how much we loved each other, and that the bond we have is unbreakable. I looked forward to being home with her, to being able to read stories with her, watch her play with her dollhouse, and to snuggle as we watched our favorite movies. She is a resilient, beautiful, strong little girl that has been through so much, and I will forever be proud of her fighting spirit during this hard time.

My expectations about welcoming baby Tug into our family were completely different than when I first found out I was pregnant. It was so hard for me to give up on the dreams I had imagined—breastfeeding, going home with my newborn for the first time, and even taking care of him by myself.

I knew those expectations needed to change and become more realistic. So, like I often do, I began thinking about the positives. I thought about how truly ecstatic I was that Tug had arrived safety. We were told that first night in the ER that we were both in incredible danger, and the fear that we would both lose our lives was all-consuming. The fact that we are both here, that we both made it through the pregnancy with minimal complications is the greatest blessing. Even though I've missed out on some things, like seeing Zoey hold her baby brother for the first time and being able to hold my baby whenever I wanted to, I knew in my heart that there would be so many other beautiful moments in our life to look forward to. In the scheme of things, I realized that nothing else mattered but that we, despite all the odds and fears, were both alive and safely together.

I've always wanted to be a mama. I quit my job as a Medical Laboratory Chemist when we moved to Seattle in 2012, so that I could spend every waking moment with my babies. It was a huge financial sacrifice for our family, and I found that staying home was a challenging job. Growing up, I was the type of person that often-judged homemakers, thinking the work was too easy. Boy, was I wrong! Each day with children can be mentally, physically, and emotionally taxing. The days are also full of opportunities to teach, inspire, and grow together. After I had Zoey, I knew I would give up any job just to be home with her. I realized my beliefs about being a homemaker were false, and I quickly learned that we can't judge others, or even begin to understand them, until we've walked in their shoes. I went from being a judgmental, childless woman, to a mama obsessed with her babies, and quickly gained an understanding of the challenges and blessings of raising children and maintaining a home.

When I got sick it was a huge adjustment and disappointment to go from being a healthy, active mom to a sick one, stuck in a hospital bed. It tested me to my limits, broke my heart, and made me long for the days where changing diapers and cleaning up messes were the highlights of my day. During those long months, I looked forward to getting back to the "real normal," including meeting the needs of my little family in small but important ways each day. I felt excited to love and kiss them around the clock, prepare their meals, read them stories, and comfort them when they cried. I wanted to keep their home safe and happy and to raise them up to be kind, loving people. Being forced to be away from my everyday life, I learned that those mundane moments are truly magical, and I never wanted to take them for granted again.

I knew that I was just at the beginning of dealing with all the emotions that would surely surface over the next days, weeks, and years. It was going to take me a long time to grieve the things cancer stole from my life. I also knew that this experience would shape me, my family, and hopefully my friends into people who could bounce back after being shoved to the ground. People who, despite the awful things that were thrown our way, still had smiles on our faces and prayers in our hearts. People who knew how to fight, every step of the way, and worked to be positive even if it was an enormous challenge to do so. People who wouldn't give up, who kept moving, even if all they could manage was an inch at a time.

We learned that even when our own expectations aren't met, God's are. He is the author of our stories, and we knew by trusting Him, everything would turn out beautifully.

CHAPTER THIRTEEN

beautiful things.

"The spirit of God hath made me, and the breath
of the Almighty hath given me life."

-Job 33:4 KJV

Two weeks after Tug's birth, I was still in the hospital, receiving my sixth round of chemotherapy. Early one morning when I couldn't sleep, I wrote about my longing to be home with my family:

It's 4:23 a.m. and I was just woken up, once again by my IV pump alarm going off. The chemo regimen I'm on, dose adjusted EPOCH-R, drips slowly at 20 ml an hour, about a drop every other second. The slow rate fills the line with bubbles, so all night long this obnoxious alarm goes off, robbing me of much needed sleep. I'm now lying here, realizing that at home my sweet baby, Tug, is probably waking up, wanting to eat, and my heart longs to be home feeding him instead of lying in this sterile hospital room dealing with an angry machine. I'm going on nine weeks in the hospital in four months. That's sixty-three nights away from home, away from my babies and my love. But luckily, I'm already on my sixth and final round, and I am praying with all my heart that this will be the end of cancer for me. It's time that I go back to being the mom I long to be: A mom who still wakes up at crazy hours in the morning, and who is just as tired—but tired from living, not from fighting this awful disease. A tired mom, who despite being exhausted herself, enjoys snuggling her beautiful babies and watching as they get to sleep peacefully.

Reading this now, it breaks my heart to know how much my family and I would still have to go through before this trial would come to an end

The weeks following Tug's birth were less intense and more enjoyable. There were no more pericardial effusions, heart drains, lymphatic fluid leaks, pregnancy symptoms and complications, or uncontrolled infections. I got a break from heart echo-grams, and my anxiety about getting Tug here safely dissipated.

I felt at the time that we were starting to get back to the way things were. I was getting stronger physically and on good days, I enjoyed going outside to soak in the sun. We even went to a Mariners vs. Red Sox game with Mike's dad! On bad days, we'd binge watch Netflix and snuggle our sweetie Tug while Zoey played make-believe with her toys in her room. I'd spend my days bathing and dressing my children, cleaning up toys, and budgeting bills—simple, everyday tasks—I loved it.

After the kids went to bed, Mike and I would talk about bills, goals, his job, and parenting. No longer was every conversation dominated by cancer—it felt amazing to talk about regular life issues once again.

Our life at that moment felt slow and easy, as if cancer had forced us to reexamine everything and go back to the beautiful basics of life. The basic things that I once took for granted but now feel are a privilege to be able to do again. I do not for one second believe that cancer is caused by God. But I truly know with all my heart, based on what I've seen and experienced, that He uses all things for good.

One of my all-time favorite worship songs is "Beautiful Things" by Gungor. The lyrics are simple, but profound. They describe that out of horrible situations, good things can and do happen, that even when we are broken and weak, God uses that to make something wonderful. He makes our pain, our mistakes, our sorrow, even our lives into something beautiful and life-changing.

One Sunday, we were attending a service at our home church in Seattle's Green Lake neighborhood. As the worship band played this song, a line of people walked to the front of the sanctuary, holding up blackboard signs. On one side of the board they wrote words that represented something bad in their lives, on the other side, what God had transformed them into. I watch, with tears rolling down my face, as person after person walked to the front, vulnerable and open, sharing the worst and best parts of their lives.

When cancer invaded our lives, I thought of that day and that song constantly. It gave me hope, knowing that although one side of my blackboard said "Cancer," the other side would show the transforming, beautiful things that God had made.

Cancer showed us that there are good people all around. We were amazed at the generosity of family, friends, and strangers alike. So many people helped us with financial donations, meals, babysitting, hospital and home visits, gifts for us and our children, car rides, and even encouraging messages left on our Facebook page made us feel incredibly loved.

Looking back, we are especially grateful for friends and family who flew up from our old home in Utah, week after week, to stay with us and help. They sacrificed their time and money to take care of us. After my treatment was over, I missed them being here. We never in our lives felt so loved and cared about as we did when I was sick.

By far, more happy tears have been shed over love and gratitude than because of pain and suffering. I could not have made it through this fight without those who loved and supported me along the way. How I wish with all my heart I could give each person who has touched our lives a giant hug. Mike and I say that the only way we'll ever be able to pay back the love and kindness is to spend the rest of our lives paying it forward. It's going to be our life mission.

One of the most beautiful things about cancer was that it forced me to see how fragile life is. Looking death straight in the eye, I realized I couldn't walk away unchanged. Part of me remains upset that my innocence about mortality was stolen. I used to walk around, never thinking about how temporary it all was. After fighting for my life, I still sometimes wish I could go back to being carefree and not think about such big things. But at the same time, I am grateful that I know what I do now.

We have seen so many beautiful things come out of our dusty story. God used this ugly cancer to create a beautiful new perspective on life for us—a new way of looking at problems and a new confidence to solve them. We realize that there are things that just aren't all that important: dirty dishes, unfolded laundry, not having enough money, worrying about buying a dream house, having the perfect career, physical appearances, the weather, traffic, and so forth. I used to have anxiety over things that truly don't matter—like whether I was spoiling Zoey by staying with her while she fell asleep every night. I look back on all the nights I felt like a bad mom and wish I could tell myself then that snuggling with my three-year-old daughter is a beautiful blessing and that one day I would sit in a hospital room dreaming about those very moments. I wish I could tell myself when I was stressing out about work or college or what to make for dinner to calm down and enjoy the moment—because everyday moments woven together are what make a beautiful life. The wonderful thing about cancer is that it cleared our minds, enabling us to see what matters most.

Cancer also brought me so much closer to my husband. He supports me, makes me laugh, kisses the tears off my face, loves my children, treats everyone with kindness and respect, never complains, and is always, always there for me. Even at the height of being exhausted and worn down from the stress of my illness, he kept a positive outlook on everything. I don't think I could love him more, but after all we have been through, I know that love has no limits.

Cancer sucks. There's no other way to put it. But the blessings that have come because of cancer have made me recognize that I have a Father in Heaven who loves extravagantly and has the power to make beautiful things out of the ugliest things. He has been with me and my loved ones every step of the way, and His Grace has transformed me. He truly is "making me new." And as crazy as it is to say, I wouldn't trade this experience for anything in the world. I can honestly say that I am grateful for all of it, the good and the bad. I think it will take me a lifetime to process everything I've learned, and to recognize all the blessings that have grown out of this "dust" that is cancer. The darkness has helped me see more clearly that life truly is beautiful and bright, and that all things can be used for good.

CHAPTER FOURTEEN

remission.

"And the God of all grace, who called you to
his eternal glory in Christ, after you have suffered
a little while, will himself restore you and make
you strong, firm, and steadfast."

-1 Peter 5: 10 NIV

Six months after my initial diagnosis, I was sitting in an exam room, Mike's hand in mine, anxiously waiting for my doctor to come into the room to deliver the news. I was so nervous and worried that the Positive Emission Tomography (PET) scan results would show that my cancer was still active and that I would need further treatment. However, my oncologist walked into the room, a huge smile on her face, the results in her hand, and declared instantly, "Well, it's all good news!" Relief swept over me. I looked over at Mike and saw his face light up with a smile that matched my own.

After going over the scan results, we walked out of the oncology wing, and Mike quickly pulled me into his arms, tears rolling down both our faces. This was the moment we had waited for since day one. The moment where I would be told that I was in remission. The moment we had been praying and hoping for with all our hearts. That hug is one I will never forget in my lifetime.

To celebrate, we went out to dinner and bought an ice cream cake, our favorite treat. Later that week, we decided to treat ourselves to a weekend getaway to Portland, Oregon. On the way down, we talked the entire time about all that we had gone through, what we had learned, and how we had changed. It was, and still is, hard to talk about some of the worst moments, such as that first week when I was told that I was at extreme risk of dying. It was heartbreaking to hear how scared Mike was and how much it hurt our Zoey to see her mama sick. It made me so sad to hear how he would break down on his drives home from the hospital after he had been so strong for me. I listened in awe at his incredible strength and determination to help and be there for me. Cancer doesn't just affect the person who is sick—their entire support team suffers too. I was so grateful for time to talk about our feelings and to really exam this journey now that things were better.

While we were in Portland, we went to the Saturday Market, where local artists display and sell their unique artwork. It was extremely hot, so we let Zoey run around in the fountains in the square. As she ran through the water in her adorable patriotic dress for the 4th of July, curly pigtails getting soaked, giggling her heart out in pure delight, I sat with Mike and Tug on the steps and just felt overcome with happiness. As I fed Tug his bottle, his eyes locked on mine, and he paused from eating to grin up at me. I looked over and caught Mike smiling at me, and I couldn't help but smile back. There were people all around us celebrating the holiday, and I felt so lucky to be out in public, doing "normal" stuff with all of them, with his beautiful family that Mike and I had created together. From my heart, I shot a prayer of gratitude up to heaven, thanking God for helping me make it to this point.

There were so many times I felt so dizzy, nauseous, tired, and in pain. There were times I was so weak that I couldn't even stand up, times I was so lonely, stuck in a tiny hospital room by myself, crying myself to sleep. There were moments I was so angry that I was sick and wondering how in the hell I was so unfortunate to get cancer at twenty-six. Moments I was so filled with fear that I wasn't going to make it and that my babies wouldn't even remember me. There were plenty of days where I had never felt so weak and fragile in my life. I can't count how many tears I've cried, or how many prayers I've said—but I will always remember the peace and comfort that followed each of those hardest moments, and the strength I felt once Grace met me where I was. God was with me the entire time, and while He didn't take the pain or heartbreak away, He filled my heart with hope, and His Grace allowed me to have joy in the midst of suffering. He strengthened my spirit when my body was weak and helped guide me out of the tremendous storm.

I wish that I could say that after I heard the good news that I was in remission that I felt complete happiness and relief. But the truth was, I still worried a lot. Every time I got a headache or a weird pain, I would worry that the cancer had returned. I was filled with anxiety and had to make a conscious effort to choose faith over fear. It wasn't easy.

I still worried that I could be in that percentage of people who didn't beat this type of cancer. However, I had one abiding reassurance. I felt that if I did die, I would have absolutely no regrets. I knew I had lived my life exactly as I wanted to and had experienced true love and joy. But I worried about the ones I would leave behind. I didn't want my loved ones to be heartbroken, or for Mike to become a widower. I wanted to be here to help raise my children and to love my husband. I wanted to spend more time with my friends and family and to love extravagantly. I wanted to make all that I'd been through mean something.

After being told I was in remission, I thought this would be my battle—learning how to live without fear and worry. Little did I know how big of a battle I was about to fight next. I would need to learn to live without fear in ways that I never would have expected, and to truly trust that no matter what, God would be there for me and my loved ones; To trust that the story He was writing with my life was so much greater than the one I could write for myself.

CHAPTER FIFTEEN

the beach.

"Be joyful in hope, patient in affliction, faithful in prayer."

-Romans 12:12 NIV

After getting approval from my oncologist that I was safe to travel, we went to visit my mom's side of the family in North Carolina. The trip was planned almost a year in advance, and when I originally got diagnosed, one of my first sad thoughts was that I would miss out on our beach vacation.

Luckily though, I was declared in "remission" in time for the trip and away we went, taking our two babies to meet their great-grandparents and all their aunts, uncles, and cousins. Because of our financial situation, my grandparents graciously offered to pay for our plane tickets, and we made it to the beach house on Topsail Island, NC.

It was a week of pure delight. We woke up every morning to the ocean waves off our back steps. Zoey would quickly get her swimsuit on, we'd lather her up in lotion, and she'd head out to the surf with whoever would grab her hand. We would shortly follow, our little Tug in our arms, dragging out beach chairs to the edge of the water, Diet Cokes in hand, sea breeze touching our face, soaking in the beautiful rays. Zoey laughed and played from sun up until she was too tired to function. She would wear herself out so much that we didn't have time to bathe her before she fell asleep in our arms, and she would wake up with her sheets covered in sand.

North Carolina has, and always will be, my heaven on earth. For a week I sat in the sun, with my two babies and my lover next me and soaked in every moment, feeling perfect peace and happiness. It was amazing to see my entire family, especially my grandparents. To be with so many loved ones at my favorite place was the perfect way to recuperate after our ordeal.

One morning, I woke up early and seized the chance to have time alone. I grabbed my "Letters to God" journal, sat on the porch steps that led to the beach, and wrote   the following:

Dear God,

As I sit here this morning, surrounded by your beauty, I feel as if my heart will burst with joy! I feel as if this is what Heaven feels and looks like.

I want to declare that I trust you. I trust that your plans for me are much greater than the ones I have for myself. You have carried me through this crazy trial, given me strength, hope, and courage when I needed it most. You have walked alongside me, never letting go.

I am amazed at your greatness and full of wonder at the

incredible miracles you have performed in my life.

People look at our family and say that we are so positive and full of hope, and I know that we are only that way because of You! It is Your strength and hope that they see! We are just vessels of your power.

Thank you for allowing me to be a lantern for your light— even though I have so many doubts and so many fears. Thank you forgiving me when I struggle to choose to trust you completely. You never give up on me!

I don't know what will happen to me, but you do, and that's enough. I do know that everything will be okay and that you will never leave my side.

Although I have fear, I also have faith—faith that no matter what happens, that grace and joy will be in those moments. You are a God of miracles; you are my everything!

I praise you. I devote my life to you. My heart overflows with love for you!
Lord Jesus, thank you for it all!

In your holy name, amen.

On our last night there, Tug was already asleep, and

somehow, I snagged Zoey in my arms and made her sit with me out on the porch. With a full moon, at high tide, waves crashing just feet below us, I sat there with my little girl in my arms, treasuring the moment. The song "Never Grow Up" by Taylor Swift came onto the radio, and I sang it to my Zoey. She finally fell asleep in my arms, and I just held her, smelling her salty-sandy hair, admiring her freckles and eyelashes, while my brother, his girlfriend, and Mike sat next to us. It was one of those nights that I felt all was right in the world, and I knew I would never forget it.

Two weeks after that beautiful night, I was back in the ER with a massive headache, receiving the terrifying news that my cancer was back, but this time in my brain. My fight was not over, and our break from reality, while enjoyable, was simply a break.

CHAPTER SIXTEEN

the golf ball.

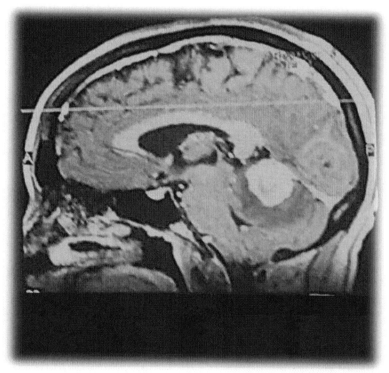

"The Lord i s m y light and m y salvation—whom
shall I fear? The Lord is the stronghold of my
life—of whom shall I be afraid?"

Psalm 27:1—NIV

The day after arriving home from our family beach trip, I started having awful headaches. Each time I would stand up, it felt as if a hammer was whacking me in the head, over and over. I would stop, close my eyes, and the feeling would pass, leaving a dull ache. I've had major migraines before, but this headache was unlike any I had ever had. I looked up the symptoms of a brain tumor, checking off the ones I had—new or worst pain ever, throbbing pain when standing, headache medicine not working, and pain worsening over time. Not sure if I was being paranoid or not, I called my oncologist to ask her what to do.

Our friends came to our house to watch the kids, and Mike took me into the ER. After dosing me up with pain meds, which helped slightly, and steroids to reduce swelling, they took me to get an MRI of my brain. A couple hours later, they came back with a black and white image, showing that I had a large tumor in my cerebellum. The ER physician told he was sorry, but I did indeed have a tumor in my brain, and they were admitting me. They wheeled me back up to the oncology floor, where I had made good friends and planned to visit, but a place I had never thought I would return to as a patient.

Getting diagnosed with cancer the first time was hard

but being told it's back is even worse. Just when I thought I was moving forward, I was ripped back to the starting line. Not even fully healed from my first fight, I was faced with a more challenging one.

The type of cancer I had, Non-Hodgkin's Primarily Mediastinal B-Cell Lymphoma (PMBCL), is extremely rare. Approximately 70,000 people a year in the United States are diagnosed with Non-Hodgkin's Lymphoma, and out of those only 2% get PMBCL. Out of that 2%, only 6% have Central Nervous System (brain and spine) involvement, roughly eighty-five people a year.

Because of the incredibly low likelihood of having brain involvement, they did not scan my head during my initial diagnosis, and it was assumed that the tumor had been there from the start.

Initially this troubled me, thinking that if it had been found earlier, it could have already been treated. The original chemo treatment for the tumor in my chest was not effective at treating my brain tumor, because it could not pass the blood-brain barrier—an amazing feature of the body. This barrier is formed by special endothelial cells that surround blood vessels in the tissues of the brain and spine. This incredible filter allows water, some gases, certain types of fats, glucose, amino acids, and other important nutrients to pass to the brain and spinal cord tissues, while simultaneously blocking certain substances from entering that could be dangerous—such as the drugs they used to treat my tumor in my chest. For this reason, I would need to receive a different type of chemotherapy, called Methotrexate. I was told that this drug should work well to eliminate the cancer. However, what they told me next showed that this was all a part of a bigger plan.

Methotrexate is a drug used for a variety of different illness and treatments, and it works by depleting the body of folic acid, which all cells (including cancer cells) need to grow and multiply. It is extremely dangerous during pregnancy because it can kill the fetus. My doctor explained to me that if they had found the brain tumor at the beginning when I was pregnant with Tug, they would have had to deliver Tug prematurely at twenty-six weeks, putting him at extreme risk of death.

I couldn't believe it—another miracle! Once again things had worked out just right. Overwhelmed, tears began pouring out of my eyes. I was so full of gratitude that Tug had been protected, and at the same time devastated that I wasn't finished fighting for my own life.

Later that day when our friends brought Zoey to see us, we tried to explain to her what was going on. We told her that I was sick again, and she asked curiously, "What happened, Mama?" We didn't know how to explain the tumor, and so we told her that I had a golf ball stuck in my head, and the doctors were going to get it out. She tilted her head, giggled, and said, "That's silly!" And off she went, running over to get the stuffed animal she had brought that day.

The plan was to receive eight treatments of Methotrexate, given every two weeks. I was warned that I would get more mouth sores, lose my hair again (which had just recently started growing), and spend a lot more time in the hospital. After I was done with the chemo, I would need whole-brain radiation and a stem cell transplant. But first I needed to get a new PICC line since they had removed my other one after I finished treatment two months prior.

The first day of chemo was uneventful. Mike brought the kids, and we fell back into living the hospital life. We had learned a few tricks to make things more enjoyable— card games for us, movies to watch on the laptop (cable TV has way too many commercials), a soft, cozy blanket (hospital blankets are so scratchy), and toys and coloring books for Zoey. I choose to wear tee shirts and gym shorts, which made me feel more comfortable. Mike helped me do what we could to make the sterile hospital room feel homier by hanging pictures of our family on the walls.

After so many stays, I grew to have a strong hatred of hospital food. Everything was so bland and way too healthy. I craved things with actual flavor, and many times, friends and family would bring me delicious meals from the outside world.

The second day of chemo was much harder, as the poisonous medicine wreaked havoc on my body. Although I wasn't nauseous, my entire body shook, I felt extremely anxious, and completely unwell. I began to cry, and my nurse came in and offered me medicine. Even though I knew that it would help give me relief, I also knew that it would end my night with my family, as I would be asleep within minutes. I began to cry, and Mike knelt in front of me. He reassured me that it was okay to take the drugs, that he didn't want me to be in so much discomfort. He gave me a hug, and I consented. The nurse gave me drugs, we said goodnight, and I slipped into a deep sleep.

The third day I woke up feeling ill, but less shaky.

Methotrexate had dropped my folic acid dangerously low, and I was given Leucovorin, also known as the "rescue drug," that would restore my levels, so I wouldn't die from treatment.

After a week off at home, I returned for a second round. Before hooking me up to chemo they ordered an MRI to check the tumor's response to the treatment. A couple hours later, my sweet nurse came into my room, sat on the edge of my bed, crying, and told me that she was so sorry, but my results were not good.

Shortly after, my oncologist came into my room, and I could tell that she had been crying too. She explained to me that the tumor in my brain was not responding to the treatment. Because of where the tumor was located, it was putting too much pressure on my spinal cord and needed to be removed as soon as possible. I was taken back to the ICU to be monitored closely.

The next day, I met the neurosurgeon, and he told me he wanted to perform surgery on me as soon as possible, but he had other patients who were in worse condition than I was that needed to be operated on first. He told me that my surgery would be very difficult, and he wanted to be very alert, and therefore I had to wait three days before it was my turn.

As each day passed, my headache worsened. Each time I stood up, it would intensify. I was confined to my bed, except for when I needed to relieve myself on the bedside commode. Anytime I bore down, the pain in the back of my head was excruciating and brought me to tears. Pain medication dulled the pain slightly, but never took away the feeling of being stabbed with a knife. For three days, my family and I sat around waiting, trying to get our minds off what was to come.

To say that I was scared about the surgery is an understatement. I was utterly terrified. The night before my surgery, I recorded my feelings:

I am having brain surgery tomorrow. I am scared I might not make it—that today may have been my last day with my amazing parents, my beautiful babies, and my loving husband. I have been savoring each moment—my hugs have been tighter than ever.

I am so upset—every ounce of me wants to live and to watch my babies grow. Every part of me loves my life. I have so much I want to do with it. I want to have more time to hold Mike's hand and to dance with him in our kitchen. I want to watch as Zoey learns how to draw her letters and pronounces everything so adorably incorrectly. I want to spend more time rocking Tug to sleep and seeing him rub his silky, soft blanket all over his face. I want to make this cancer story into the purpose of my life, to help others make it through their struggles, and to mourn with those who mourn. I can't wait to be healthy again and to be that person who gives someone a hug when they most need it, like I've been given.

I am scared, but I am also so hopeful. I am amazed at the people around me. The doctors and nurses who are doing everything they can to keep me safe and happy. I am blown away at the generosity and kindness of strangers. I am grateful for the prayers that people have sent up to heaven for us. We have felt each and every one of them, and we know God works miracles. In the past six months, we have seen His hands in every aspect of our lives, and we know without a doubt He will be there tomorrow for us too.

When I think about all that could go wrong, it scares me beyond belief. The "what-ifs" break my heart and make me want to curl up and hide from it all. I know I have to stop going there—because the truth is, since day one of this cancer journey, I have had a lot of "what ifs." And more times than not, things have turned out better than I had expected.

God's grace has been in every moment, both good and bad, throughout this entire fight. His hand has been guiding us and directing us, unfolding this beautiful, miraculous story of hope. I feel blessed that He has chosen our little family to share His power with—to show that there can be happiness in the middle of suffering, and that we as human beings are capable of so much more strength and courage than we ever thought possible. I believe with all my heart that the story God writes with our lives is so much greater than the one we could write on our own. I trust Him with my life, and I trust Him with the lives of my children, Mike, my parents, brother and sisters, and all my many loved ones. He has been here for me, and He will be there for each one of us, if only we let Him. His Grace is sufficient for all. Even in the hardest times, good times can be had. We must never ever give up hope that life is good, meaningful, and worth fighting for.

I pray with all my heart that the surgery goes well tomorrow, and that this is the last major hurdle towards a cancer-free life. I sure hope that God knows that I plan on using this story for good. Each waking moment of my life will be to show that God makes beautiful things out of the dust.

I pray that the surgeon's hands will be guided and protected, and that I will have a lifetime left of love to give to those people all around me. All my faith and all my hope is in the One who gives life, who brings healing and love to this earth, and whose grace covers all.

CHAPTER SEVENTEEN

peace.

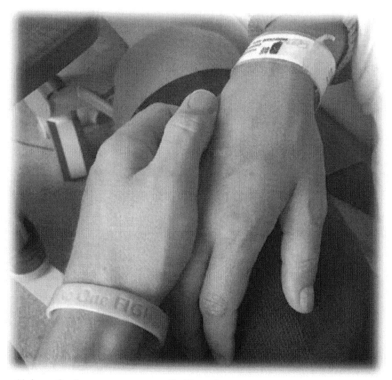

"And the peace of God, which passeth all understanding, shall keep your hearts and minds through Christ Jesus."

-Philippians 4:7 NIV

139

Before my brain surgery, I was terrified because I knew exactly what they were going to do to me. From my time as a surgical tech, I knew how complex brain surgery could be. Just like when I had my C-section, I hated the idea that I would be the one on the table and not the one passing instruments.

As we were waiting for the surgical team to get ready, I shared my fears with my dad, and as he always does, he gave me advice. My dad is not a religious man, but he does believe in something bigger and a life beyond. He has always been someone I can go to for advice, and in that moment, I needed him more than anything. He told me that if I felt like I was being pulled to the next side, to fight and to come back.

During my ten-hour brain surgery, there were two times when I knew I was dying. I struggle to find the words to explain what I felt because it is nearly indescribable. I remember looking down at my right hand and seeing another hand in mine. We were walking towards a brilliant light together, and it was just so incredibly beautiful. I have never felt so much love, peace, and happiness. To be honest, I really wanted to go.

I remember a voice asking me if I wanted to stay or go.

I knew it was the Savior holding my hand and asking me this obvious question. Of course, I wanted to go! It was so beautiful, so peaceful, so full of love—and I didn't want to hurt anymore. I wanted to be with Him.

As we walked hand-in-hand, I remembered what my dad had said and the life I would be leaving behind. I thought of my children, my sweetheart, my friends and family—and twice I chose to return. Thank God I did! I still have so much more life to live! So many people to love, places to explore, things to learn.

When I woke up from surgery, both my dad and Mike were by my bed, holding my hands, smiling at me with tears in their eyes. I felt relieved and grateful, knowing that I had made the right choice.

I was happy I chose to live, but I will never forget the feeling I had as my Savior held my hand and gently led me. I will never forget the absolute peace and the pure love I felt. I look forward to being there when my life is complete, but I am so grateful for the opportunity to still be here on this beautiful earth with my beautiful people.

I believe in a Heaven that offers freedom from pain and sorrow. This belief has erased my worries of my own death—I have almost been there, and I promise there is nothing to fear! There is only joy and happiness, peace and grace. The glimpse of Heaven I had during this awful surgery filled me with hope and courage to live a life full of meaning. I will forever be grateful I was given more time and for the eternity that awaits.

A few days after my surgery, I wrote in my journal:

"*Dear God,*

This week I had a ten-hour brain surgery and I made it! I was really scared I was going to die, that all my fears were going to come true. In the middle of the surgery, I felt you. I even felt you taking me **home**. *I wasn't scared. I was at peace. I loved being with you. I knew that coming back to earth was going to be hard—and it has been. I am really fighting right now to get strong again, have courage, and feel peace. But I am alive! I was so close, but I chose to stay. My biggest fear—that my family wouldn't be alright without me was a lie! They are always going to be okay because they have You! Heavenly Father, when I was afraid, your gentle arms wrapped tightly around me—you pulled me in tight, and made me feel secure, safe, and loved. You* showed me that you hold my loved ones like you hold me. I don't need to worry about my family anymore—I give you everything I have Lord, even them.

Jesus, my hands are empty, and my heart is yours.

In Your Holy Name, Amen."

CHAPTER EIGHTEEN

hard work.

"The righteous cry out, and the Lord hears them;
he delivers them from all their troubles. The Lord
is close to the broken-hearted and saves those
who are crushed inspirit."

-Psalm 34:17-18 NIV

Out of all the things I had been through—chemotherapy, blood transfusions, heart drains, C-section delivery, staph infections, —recovering from brain surgery hit my emotional core like no other. Besides the occasional headache, I was not in pain, but my coordination and balance were gone and fighting to get them back brought me both to tears and to my knees countless times.

For the first week, I was so dizzy that I couldn't even see straight. I would try and look at something and my vision was all over the place. I felt so trapped, lying in bed, not being able to even read or watch television. I would turn on podcasts or music and just fall asleep. When people visited, I was in such a mental fog from the surgery and from the pain meds that I couldn't remember having coherent conversations with them. To make matters worse, during the surgery, I bit off part of my tongue and had thrush all over in my mouth, making it extremely painful to talk or eat. I hated that I couldn't even communicate. I had never felt so trapped or lonely in my life.

Day by day in the months that followed, things slowly started to improve. I worked really hard to be independent again and to be able to take care of my children. My "physical therapy" was doing things like laundry, dishes, dressing the kids, organizing closets, taking showers by myself, and going for walks holding onto someone or something. My muscles were so weak from being bedridden that they burned each night as if I was training for a marathon. I would think back to all the times I got annoyed having to do all the things a parent is required to do—getting the kids dressed and fed, keeping them entertained. Those became the things I would dream about doing, like carrying my six-month-old across the room without fear of dropping him or walking with my daughter to the park.

My heart remains absolutely overwhelmed with gratitude towards my army of helpers during this time, especially my sister, who dropped her life for me, moved into our two-bedroom apartment, and became our full-time caregiver. She cooked, cleaned, held my hand as I walked, never complained that I couldn't help, played with her niece and nephew, drove me to all my appointments, binge watched Netflix with me, and was always there to listen. I will never be able to pay her back for her countless acts of selfless love, but I will forever hold a special place in my heart for those moments where the brilliance of sisterhood shown the brightest between us.

Cancer is not just about the patient fighting—it takes an entire army. Sometimes I felt like I had the easy job because I could literally sit and ask my helpers to do everything for me. It was a very humbling experience, and one that I often felt uncomfortable with. I am a pretty independent, self-driven person and to accept help was challenging for me. It took me awhile to realize that others wanted to help me and that I wasn't a burden to them after all. I got better at asking for help, but in the back of my mind I was always thinking of ways that I could repay their kindness, to show gratitude and not just speak it.

There were so many hard days during my recovery. Many times before lying down for a nap, I would read scriptures and fall into bed crying. I wanted this trial to be over. Although I believed with all my heart that God was there, and there was a purpose to this suffering, I was still sad. I felt heartbroken every day that this was our life. Why us? We had the happiest, cutest life before this. It was simple. We barely had enough to get by, but we had lots of fun, and we took really good care of each other. We always were and are nice to people. We always try our best to be good citizens.

During my near-death experiences, I was given a

chance to look back at my life. I saw all the people I loved, and that's what made me want to come back. I knew going back would be hard, but I knew that I was meant to be here a little bit longer, and that sweet Jesus led me with his gentle hand back. Most importantly, He let me choose. Knowing that I chose to live made it possible for me to get through those nearly impossible days. It gave me the strength to fight for my life and to fight for my future as a "normal" wife, mother, sister, daughter, and friend.

The truth is that life is messy, and good people get sick. Bad things happen to good people, and good things happen to bad. It doesn't mean we should stop being nice or kind or good. It especially means that we shouldn't stop believing that God is on our side, that He loves us, and wants the best for us.

I believe that the human spirit can overcome all obstacles, that people are resilient, and that joy can win. But the truth was that I had so many moments of anger, where I have cried out with pure rage. I was upset and furious. I wasn't happy all the time. I'm human, and in those hard days, weeks, and months, I was hurting.

As much as I hate that my cancer returned, I feel like it was God's way of helping me understand that life is a choice. Each day we choose to make something out of our lives. Even though I felt frustrated at my body, I also felt proud of it each day for working so hard. No matter how hard it got, I'm grateful that God gave me a second chance. I like to think I got cancer again so that when all of this was said and done, I could live more fearlessly and with a surety that everything would be alright.

CHAPTER NINETEEN

radiation.

"… Do not grieve, for the joy of the
LORD is our strength."

-Nehemiah 9:10 NIV

The original plan to treat my brain tumor was chemo, radiation, and then a stem cell transplant. Adding brain surgery in the middle made everything more complicated. After surgery, my doctors wanted me to have as much time to recover as possible, so they decided to push back the radiation. Earlier that year, my best friend that I've known since preschool planned a trip to come visit us from Utah. We have always had in common our love of nature, and I was so excited to share my beautiful Pacific Northwest with her. She booked the tickets, and shortly after I found out about the tumor in my brain. She decided that she still wanted to come up and be with me.

She arrived a couple of days after I got home from my surgery, and I was a mess. So dizzy and unbalanced, unable to communicate properly, so tired and worn out. She went with me to see my oncologist for a check-up. When I told my doctor that I was having more headaches, she decided I needed to be admitted to the ICU, concerned that the fluid on my brain was building back up, my tumor was growing, and I would need another surgery. She determined that I needed to start radiation right away.

Once again, I was back in the ICU. I was disappointed that I was incapable of living the life I wanted to and upset that I couldn't spend time having fun—that I was once again confined to a hospital bed. However, my friend understood. She too has major health challenges and knows the frustration that results when our bodies don't respond how we want them too. Having her there was a relief—my best friend, my maid of honor at my wedding, was with me and understood how I felt. Once again, I understood that God had placed her in my life for many reasons, this being one of the greatest.

The next day they woke me up early and rolled me to the oncology radiation department. In the room there was a large machine that looked similar to an MRI machine. The radiation technologist helped me scoot from my hospital bed over to the thin, cold table.

Since lymphoma spreads easily in the brain and it's hard to pinpoint exactly where to target, I received Whole Brain Radiation. This is often considered a curable treatment to brain lymphoma since it is so effective at killing every single cancer cell in the brain tissues. This treatment is risky though—it can often cause brain damage, early dementia, and other cognitive issues—but due to my young age, the benefits outweighed the risks.

To ensure the safety of the procedure, they needed to

prevent radiation from missing the target, and to ensure precision, they needed to make a special mask for me. This mask would go over my face and bolt my head down to the table, preventing me from moving while the radiation beams shot through my head.

As I laid on the table, one radiation technologist stood next to my bed, laying her hand on my arm, comforting me. The other technologist came over, showing me the plastic mesh material she was going to be putting on my face to create a cast. She dipped it into a water basin on the table next to her, lifted it up, asked me if I was ready, and after confirming that I was, she pushed it down over my face, locking me to the table.

Instantly I started to panic. I'm not usually claustrophobic, but this made me feel so. To get my mind off the sticky mask that was suffocating me, I tried meditating, imagining that I was walking on a sandy pathway, smelling the sea breeze, feeling the long strands of grass brushing my fingertips, and finally seeing the ocean waves crashing on the shore as I reached the other side of the dunes.

The cast finally dried, they unbolted it from the table, and pulled it slowly from my skin. They both congratulated me, telling me that this was tough for most people, and I had done great.

Later that day, after the mask was dry, they took me back again to get my first radiation treatment. My oncology radiologist had told me that I would get around twenty-one doses of radiation. He also explained what symptoms and side effects could occur: major fatigue, permanent hair loss, and headaches from swelling.

My first two treatments were done while I was an inpatient. I was very nervous for the first one, remembering the feeling I had when the mask was being made. They got me on the table, placed the mask on my face, and again I forced myself to the beach. The entire procedure took about eight minutes and went better than expected. I was released from the hospital, and each morning following, Mike drove me to my treatments, while my sister stayed home with my babies. Even though I would rather have gone out for breakfast or something, it kind of felt like we were having a date. During the thirty-minute ride to and from the hospital, we had time alone to talk and connect, and for that I was grateful. After a quick fifteen-minute appointment, we headed back home, Mike went into work, and I would climb back into bed.

The radiation made me extremely exhausted. There were many times I slept the entire day while my sister took care of my kids. I was so grateful for her help—she's such an amazing aunt, and Zoey and Tug had a lot of fun spending their days with her.

In addition to being tired, the skin on my scalp felt as if it had been sunburned, and I constantly had to use radiation burn gel to soothe it. My hair began to fall out again, and after getting tired of waking up to a furry pillow, I had Mike shave my head. This time was more fun—he cut my hair into a mohawk, colored it red with hair markers, and styled it. Next, I pulled out my black star earrings, put on lots of black makeup and a black tee shirt, and I posed as a rock star for a picture. We had a good laugh, I cried a bit, and he hugged me tight before continuing to shave the remaining hair.

At the time I was optimistic that my hair loss would be temporary, but over time I've realized it is gone forever. The radiation had destroyed all but a few hair follicles, and I was going to be bald for the rest of my life. I knew this was going to be a lifelong challenge for me—accepting that a part of me would always be missing. But I also knew that I would give up my hair any day, knowing that in return I would still have my life.

Since then, I have gone through some interesting challenges. I've learned that people can be super awkward when they don't understand, so to clear the air I just flat out tell them. I joke about my wigs and explain how much fun it is to experiment with new looks. I also tell them that they are itchy, and I miss my old hair. I'm upfront and honest, and I find that people feel more comfortable after I show them that I'm okay.

My last day of radiation became one of my favorites. I enjoyed my time with Mike, but it did take a lot of energy to get up so early to get treatment, and I looked forward to having more relaxing mornings. After they took my mask off for the last time, they congratulated me, gave me hugs, and walked me out to the hallway. One of the technologists gave me a mallet, and took me to the other side of the hallway, where a gong hung from the wall with a poem hanging above it:

"Strike this gong,

For you have been strong,

It's tone to clearly say,

My treatment is done,

This course is run,

And I am on my way."

I looked over at Mike, saw that he was smiling from ear to ear, and smiled back. I hit that brass gong hard, and the tune was overshadowed by cheers from the many people surrounding me. This chapter of my story was finally over. I was one step closer to the finish line, and it felt incredible!

CHAPTER TWENTY

transplant.

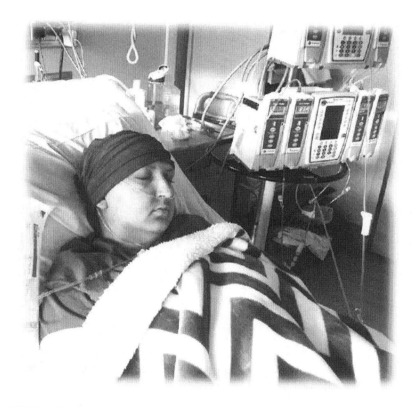

"The LORD himself goes before you and will be with you; he will never leave you nor forsake you. Do not be afraid; do not be discouraged."

-Deuteronomy 31:8 NIV

After radiation, I needed an autologous stem cell transplant to give me the best chance of survival. In a nut shell, my immune system would be killed and brought back to life. The doctors brought out the diagrams and explained to me how the stem cells were going to replace my unhealthy blood-forming cells with new healthy cells.

Before I could get the transplant, I had to undergo many tests and procedures: dental exams, a lumbar puncture, a bone marrow biopsy, MRI and CT scans, tons of blood work, lung function tests, and more. I had a special IV placed called a Hickman, similar to a PICC line, just more heavy duty. The entire week before the transplant I had to give myself GSF shots in order to mass produce blood products for collection. The shots weren't fun, but the pressure and pain in every single one of my bones as the cells grew rapidly were even worse.

After I was deemed "ready," my stem cells were harvested. This was done by hooking me up to a machine that pumped my blood out of my body and into a filtering machine that collected the stem cells and returned my blood back to me. It took over four hours a day, two days in a row to collect over four million stem cells! They were sent to storage, preserving them until I was ready to receive them. I found it all incredibly intriguing.

I was at the Seattle Cancer Care Alliance (SCCA) clinic almost daily for a month. I was so tired and emotionally worn out, wanting so badly to be home with my family. Instead I was stuck in waiting room chairs, surrounded by other cancer patients who looked like they were feeling the same way I was. A week before Thanksgiving, I was admitted to the UW Medical Center to begin the transplant process. It started with nine days of chemotherapy, all potent and full of fun side effects. The first drug I received (Thiotepa) made me extremely nauseous, and because it seeped out through the pores of my skin I as required to take sponge baths four times a day. This was difficult because I was always cold, tired, and weak and getting up was a real chore. The second drug (Busulfan) gave me an awful brown rash (nicknamed the "Busulfan Tan") all over my body that made my skin itchy and painful. It was disturbing to see layers upon layers of my skin falling off every time I touched it. The final drug (Cytarabine) made my face feel as if it was on fire during the entire four-hour infusion.

By the end of the week, I had mucositis—open sores in the mouth, throat, and rest of the digestive track.

It was extremely painful to talk. To help, my nurses had me swish my mouth with a concoction of antibiotic, anesthetic, antifungal, corticosteroid, and antacid they called "magic mouthwash." Going to the bathroom was also extremely painful, and I was given a paste with three different diaper rash creams and lidocaine, called "Boston Butt Paste." My entire body was under attack.

After finishing chemo, I had one day off to rest before my transplant. I was relieved to be done with what I thought would be the hardest part and excited for the next stage. In the transplant community, transplant day is considered our "New Birthday," and to me it sounded like it was going to be good—I was wrong.

The next day, the transplant nurses came into my room, and after verifying my identity, they pulled a small red bag from a locked cooler, hung it up on my IV stand and slowly, drip by drip, they transfused the stem cells into me.

Shortly after starting the drip, a nurse gave me an orange slice and told me to suck on it. I was confused. She explained that the preservatives used to keep the stem cells alive made people fairly nauseous. Fairly was a huge understatement.

I threw up more than I ever had in my life. My stomach hurt so bad that I felt like someone was stabbing me. I could hear the guy in the room next to mine screaming, "I'm dying! I'm dying!" He was getting his stem cells at the same time, and I knew exactly what he meant. It was horrific. The transfusion was slow, and because I had not eaten for a few days because of mucositis, all I had to throw up was the green bile from the bottom of my stomach. Since we had not anticipated that this would be a painful experience, Mike had gone to work that day. I wept in between vomiting, wishing for the time to go faster. I desperately wanted Mike to be there holding me, comforting me. Instead I was alone with strangers.

Later that day, the sores that were covering my mouth began to really hurt. It was so painful that when Mike showed up with the kids, I could barely talk. I had been looking forward all day to their visit, and when it arrived, I was in too poor of condition to enjoy it, making my spirits fall even further. I had expected this day to be a good one, and it had turned out to be one of my worst.

I was told that after receiving the stem cells it would take ten to fourteen days for them to engraft or begin to grow and make healthy blood cells. During this time, I had absolutely no immune system, which put me at extreme risk of infection. I was also at risk for extreme bleeding, becoming anemic, having my vital organs (such as heart, lungs, liver, and kidney) severely damaged, and developing nutritional problems.

Until my immune system was back, I had labs drawn daily to check my blood counts. Often, I would receive plasma and red blood cell transfusions. I couldn't eat anything due to the mucositis throughout my entire digestive track, so I received all my nutrition through my IV. Each day, bags of fluid filled with glucose, salts, amino acids, lipids, vitamins and minerals were pumped into my body. When I had loose bowel movements, they automatically treated me as if I had a contagious illness called C. Diff. Colitis. Each time it happened (which was often), my room was marked with a bright "isolation area" sign on the door. That sign meant that everyone who entered my room was required to wear a gown, mask, and gloves. It was impossible to enforce the rule on our kids, so those days they stayed home—making me feel even more isolated. This was done to prevent the spread of the infection to other patients until lab results confirmed that I was C. Diff. free.

Each day the cells began to double, and after what felt like years, my blood count finally reached the magic number that indicated that the cells had engrafted—a very huge milestone in the transplant process. From there, my cells began to grow rapidly, and I moved into a safe zone with my brand new immune system.

I was told that I had the immunity of a brand-new baby. I would have to be extra cautious with foods and try my best to stay away from others with any kind of illness. When I reached my "first birthday," I would need to get all my childhood vaccines again.

Just as I was gearing up to be discharged from the hospital, I started going downhill again. It became increasingly difficult to breathe, my oxygen levels dropped, and I began coughing up an immense amount of nasty colored mucous. I was taken to get a CT scan to view my lungs, and when results came back, it was confirmed that I had bacterial pneumonia. I felt so disappointed, knowing that my stay would be extended, and began to cry. Again, Mike was at work, and I had to deal with the bad news on my own.

They started me on heavy doses of antibiotics before they knew the exact type of pneumonia I had. They told me the next morning that they would need to do a bronchoscopy, and I panicked. A bronchoscopy is a procedure where a scope is used to view the inside of the lungs and to take a biopsy for further analysis. Again, because of my scrub tech days, I knew too much.

Mike was at work, so I called my dad, crying to him over the phone, telling him how terrified I was. I didn't expect it to hurt—I was just really freaked out. I knew that they would give me just enough medications to make me loopy, but I would still be awake; that they would put a block in my mouth so that they could push the long tube down my throat, and I couldn't cough. I knew that I would feel the pain of the needle as they took a small bite out of my lung for the biopsy. I wept uncontrollably, and my dad said everything he could to calm me down.

Fortunately, Mike was able to get off work and be there in time for the procedure. First, I was given a breathing treatment, containing steroids and anesthetics. It slowly numbed my throat and mouth. Then they gave me some narcotics, so the pain wouldn't bother me. Having Mike there calmed me down the most, and after saying a prayer with me, he sat in the chair next to me, holding onto my hand tightly.

To my surprise, the procedure was easy and quick. It was weird feeling the tube poking around in my chest, and it stung for a second when they took the biopsy. But other than that, it was a piece of cake. I had worked myself up too much, and let my imagination get out of control.

The biopsy results showed that it was a common, curable bacterial pneumonia. With the help of meds and lots of fluid, it would resolve over time. Meanwhile, they would continue to monitor me. I still had so many mouth sores, and to manage the pain they made me swish with saline and more "Magic Mouthwash." Respiratory therapists were continually checking on me, adjusting the amount of oxygen given through nasal cannulas that were hard and uncomfortable. I had awful headaches, due to my lack of oxygen, and because they wanted to monitor me for signs of a fever, I couldn't take regular pain medication like Tylenol, and instead was given heavier stuff, like Oxycodone. If I had a headache, I could choose to be in pain, or to sleep—neither of which I wanted to do.

I could feel my muscles deteriorating from lack of movement. Getting out of bed became extremely hard. Upon standing I would feel dizzy and weak. I had to call the nurse each time I needed to go to the bathroom, so they could supervise me as I took a single step out of bed, turned around, and sat down on the bedside commode. It was so embarrassing having another person take of my waste and cleaning up after me.

Physical therapists came to my room each day to take me on walks, which lasted barely a few minutes before I would need to sit down and rest. Everything was hard and frustrating, and I felt trapped by my circumstances.

CHAPTER TWENTY-ONE
depressed.

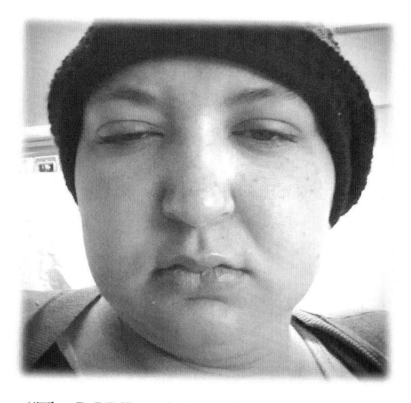

"The LORD upholds all who fall and lifts up all who are bowed down."

-Psalm 145:14 NIV

Over the next few weeks, I recovered from the bacterial pneumonia. I was almost ready to start eating again, my strength was building, and my immune system was getting stronger each day. I was convinced I would be home for Christmas, but just as I got well from one type of pneumonia, I was brought right back down with a different type. This time with cryptogenic organizing pneumonia (COP). There is no known cause for this illness and it's not contagious, but it is just as dangerous as other types of pneumonias. It's treated with heavy, long-term doses of Prednisone, a steroid anti-inflammatory. Once again, I was struggling to breathe, continually hooked to monitors and oxygen tanks. I was heartbroken when they told me it would be a couple more weeks before I could go home. I would be spending the holidays in that cold, dark hospital room.

The side effects of chemo, the awful symptoms of pneumonia, the pain meds making me dazed and constantly tired, and the steroids that made it impossible to sleep were rough. But the worst was the loneliness. Hours upon hours of being alone, confined to a bed, not feeling well enough to even go to the bathroom without the help of a nurse. I missed my family so bad that I spent hours going through my phone over and over looking at pictures of them. I had visitors, but only here and there; the UW Medical Center is kind of far from our home and not super kid—friendly. FaceTime helped, but it was hard to connect with Zoey and Tug through a screen.

The loneliness tortured me. Even though a nurse would come in every four hours for twenty minutes or so, I had way too much time to think and way too much time alone doing nothing. There were nights I was so sad, so scared, and so afraid that I secretly prayed that I would not wake up in the morning. I can't believe I ever felt that way, after how hard I had fought, after all I had survived. I had everything to live for, yet at some moments I wanted to die. That's how sick and sad I was.

I was depressed. It finally caught up to me: the months and months of treatment; all the traumatizing things that had happened to me. All the scary moments, all the sad ones; the things I had missed and wouldn't get back—like being home with my infant son during his first year of life. I stopped enjoying anything and cried over everything. I prayed all the time. I wasn't quite suicidal, but I got so low that I felt like it would be easier to go than to fight—and that really scared me.

After a couple of days of non-stop crying, I asked to speak with the Psychiatry team, and they saved my life. They talked with me about my feelings and said that they were shocked that I hadn't felt that way earlier, that most cancer patients get anxiety or depression. I also talked with a pastor from our church, and he reminded me that God has always used the weakest and most unlikely heroes to tell his story of Grace; that even the most valiant characters of the Bible had flaws; that it was okay to be angry at God that I had cancer; that I could talk to Him about it. I also talked with the chaplain, and she suggested I hadn't given myself time to grieve and maybe I should just cry. I started on a prescription and began to pray more sincerely. The combination of therapy, medication, and faith saved me.

Even though the transplant process was awful, there were bright moments. When my family did come to visit, I would hold my babies and smell their hair. I would color with Zoey and rock baby Tug to sleep. I would try and stand to give Mike a lingering hug. When they were there, I forgot that my life was so hard. I could remember why I was fighting and why I had to survive. These three people in my life mean more to me than anything, and it's hard to comprehend that I even felt the urge to stop fighting for them.

But that's how mental health works. It is an illness too, and it needs to be viewed that way. It can't be taken lightly or ignored. My depression gave me a new understanding of the many people I love who suffer with this disease. I now understand it's not something you can just "snap out of." It comes on unexpectedly, and sometimes you need help to get out of it. It is just as dangerous as any other illness. I didn't understand it before. Now I do.

Back to the good things. I got to meet Seahawks players, which made Mike super jealous. I met the most amazing nurses who instead of running when I was upset gave me hugs and encouragement. I became friends with my darling housekeeper, and on my last day I left her a note and was able to hug her goodbye. I received beautiful cards of encouragement from friends and family. I wasn't eating well, so my doctor brought me Cheez-Its. Another CNA brought me coloring pages and her favorite orange MIO water enhancer and would sit in my room at night and talk with me when she could. I had good talks with my dad and others on the phone.

Even though I was stuck in the hospital for Christmas,

Mike decorated my room with a mini tree and lights, and we had a small family Christmas in room 8214. During this time, I didn't have to worry about my children because I knew they were either with their aunt or Mike, both who love and protect them unconditionally.

Once I got help for my depression, things gradually improved. One of the most memorable things about that time in the hospital was that each night, even though I felt sad and lonely, I never felt like I was alone. There were so many nights I would look over at the chair, convinced that someone was there watching over me. I felt the presence of angels and loved ones, especially my late grandma and aunt. I would wake up so sure someone was there, but the chair was always empty. It helped on those pitch-dark nights when I lost hope. I have a hard time finding the right words to explain, but it was beautiful.

On one of those dark nights, several weeks into my stay, I recorded my feelings:

I am praying with all my heart that in a couple weeks after yet another MRI of my brain, I am once again declared in remission, and this time, for real. I hope with all my heart I get to live the rest of my life cancer-free, and that I can use this awful, beautiful story to spread hope, and encourage others. I want to be here to help raise my children and love my husband. I can honestly say that after what I've been through, I do trust God. I want to be fearless and not worry about the small stuff. I want to hand over my problems instantly to my Savior. The truth is that there are no small moments in our lives. Everything that happens to us has a purpose and we can turn it into something beautiful with His help. Cancer has really kicked our butts, but it also blessed us immensely, and I am glad it's our story. I'll be even gladder when it's all over.

My nurse today said that everyone's life seems to be full of storms, and that when one storm ends, another one starts. And I must agree with her. Life is hard. Not just for me right now—everyone has their own battle. We don't always know the battles people are fighting, and so I want to make sure that I am always kind to and thoughtful of others. Maybe they are hiding their depression. Let's all be kind. Grace goes a long way, and I have been lucky to receive so much of it. I'm going to have to spend the rest of my entire life "paying it forward," and I pray I get that opportunity.

After spending six and half weeks (two times longer

than originally scheduled) at UWMC, I was finally able to go home. I was finally able to do art projects with my Zoey, rock my sweet giggly Tug, and hug Mike as often as I wanted to. It was so good to be home because I got to see the ordinary day happening, which was extraordinary. I got see Zoey dancing when Elmo came on the television, and I was there when Tug learned to crawl and get into everything. We even threw Zoey a little birthday party! Every night, I helped Mike put the kids to bed then curled up on the couch with him to watch one of our shows we liked and eat ice cream. Being home with my family in our cozy little apartment—toys cluttering the floor, dirty dishes in the sink, and laundry baskets overfilling with clothes was exactly where I wanted to be.

CHAPTER TWENTY-TWO
He is Risen!

"He is not here: for he is risen as he said. Come,
see the place where the Lord lay."

-Matthew 28: 7 KJV

The week before Tug's first birthday, I had an MRI done on my brain as a checkup. My doctor called to tell me she was really concerned about new growth and that I had to see the brain oncologist at Seattle Cancer Care Alliance as soon as possible. I got off the phone and broke down sobbing. Coincidently, my sister dropped by for a visit at that exact moment and sat with me until Mike got home. When he arrived, we went into the other room, so we wouldn't frighten the kids, and he held me in his arms as we both cried our eyes out. We were both consumed with absolute fear and worry, so terrified that the cancer was back, and we would have to start all over again going through treatment that most likely wasn't going to be very effective.

Instead of staying home and worrying all weekend, we decided to go to one of our favorite places and find some peace. We quickly packed up our car and drove to Seaside, Oregon to stay at the beach. We stayed off our phones and spent the entire weekend loving one another and praying. The entire four-hour drive down to Seaside, tears rolled down my face. I just couldn't stop crying, convinced that this time might be the last go-around for me.

Mike and I couldn't help but soak in every moment,

thinking they might be "the last time." We held each other tighter and talked about all the amazing memories we'd created together. We snuggled with our children and played with them on the swing set on the beach. Lenka, our golden retriever, ran around in the sand and water, tail wagging a million miles per minute, with a huge puppy grin on her face.

The weather was perfect. There was only a slight breeze, beautiful blue skies, and the sun was shining brightly. The magnificent ocean waves crashing off shore and the sea breeze was enough to calm our souls and give us the peace we needed to deal with whatever might come next.

On Easter morning, Zoey woke us up super early, and we watched as our darling girl ran around the room excitedly hunting for her eggs and treats from the Easter bunny. One of her gifts was a set of children's Bible stories, and we read the story of Easter together. After we explained to her that Jesus had Risen and that was why we celebrated the holiday—Zoey was upset that she couldn't see him in real-life. It was an interesting concept to teach a four-year-old, so we explained to her that He still lives—just in our hearts.

After the gifts were found and the eggs accounted for the kids took a nap. Mike and I sat looking out at the ocean. I looked over, and noticed he was crying, so I went over, climbed into his lap, and cried with him. No words were spoken between us—we already knew how the other felt: fear, sadness, anger, heartbreak, and worry. But we held each other, foreheads touching, whispering "I Love You's" to each other.

We had been together for over eleven years, and I knew this man loved me unconditionally. He had sure seen the worst and best of me—there was nothing that wasn't known between us. He has always been my best friend, and we've had so many fun adventures, the greatest of which has been becoming parents together. Not once in my lifetime have I had my heart broken by the man I love—how lucky am I? How rare is that?! Pretty neat if you ask me.

After the kids woke up, we packed up our hotel and headed down to the beach for one last session on the swing sets. Lenka ran around, and Zoey squealed with delight, "Daddy, Push Me Higher!" Little Tug was wrapped up in the baby carrier inside my jacket, giggling at his sister and dad. I watched them all with a big smile across my face, soaking it all in. Mike looked up and noticed I was smiling at them, and he grinned back at me.

We finally got Zoey off the swings and gathered together. We all hugged each other and said a prayer on the beach. We thanked the Lord for all our many blessings and answered prayers, asking for His help to get through whatever was to come.

It was the most beautiful Easter I have ever had. The combination of the love we felt for each other, God's beautiful creation all around us, amazing weather, and the spirit of Christ was incredible. I'll never forget how close we all felt to each other and to our Savior in that moment. It truly was a gift. A memory worth keeping forever.

We drove home, and the next day my dad and Mike went with me to my brain oncology appointment, while my sister babysat my kids. We were all so tense and worried but tried to keep our anxieties under control.

The doctor pulled up the images and compared my most recent scan to the last one from three months prior. When he said, "Oh, this spot's new," all our hearts dropped. Mike said he felt like crying, and I was stunned. This could not be happening.

But as the doctor looked at the images, it became clear

to him that the spot on my brain scan was actually a small brain bleed and not lymphoma. Overwhelming relief flooded over us, smiles brightening all our faces. Only for a cancer patient would the words "only a small brain bleed," be good news—we were ecstatic!

We left SCCA filled with hope, light, and joy. My heart was full of gratitude, as I thanked my Father in Heaven for the good news.

It was an awful experience to go through, thinking that it might be the end. But despite our agonizing fear, we held on tighter and loved deeper. If we learned anything that Easter weekend, it's that we should live that way always. For life is a gift, and no one knows when theirs will be taken away. We should love people at all times, and in all places, never ceasing to show our gratitude.

The next day we celebrated Tug's birthday. There was a time along our path when I didn't think this day would happen. After watching him devour his first birthday cake, we cleaned him up, and I held him while he fell asleep in my arms, his long eyelashes batting over his ocean blue eyes—thinking to myself, oh how great is our Lord!

CHAPTER TWENTY-THREE
sea legs.

"We have this hope as an anchor for the soul, firm and secure."

-Hebrews 6:19 NIV

The summer of 2016 flew by. We had so much fun wearing ourselves out enjoying life. Mike had a slower work schedule, I had fewer doctor's appointments, and we had long summer days to spend in the Pacific Northwest. We visited Utah for a couple of weeks to see our family, the first time since I was diagnosed. We went to a few weddings, some of our friends had babies, and we spent time with other friends and family.

After the crazy year we had, we decided it was a no brainer that our family needed to make some good memories together. We bought a small, tear-drop camper, and went camping as often as we could.

To say we weren't tired most of the time is an understatement. We were purely exhausted—from chasing Tug around and getting angry at him for climbing on top of the kitchen table and trying to jump off at only 17 months old to; doing art projects everyday with Zoey, because like her mama, she's got the desire to create something every single moment of her day; cleaning up spilled milk or running to the grocery store for more milk because we never had enough. Tug was having night terrors, and would wake up screaming, making for tough nights. Zoey was in the "why stage" and never stopped talking. She had so many questions, and we simply did not have enough answers to satisfy our curious little girl.

We were so tired from our simple, amazing, extraordinary life—and I didn't want to change a thing. At night when we finally got the kids in bed, Mike and I would sit on the couch, glued, so physically and mentally exhausted but feeling full of joy, knowing we were exactly where we wanted to be.

The year before, I was having a major operation to remove the tumor in my brain. Everyone thought I was done. I could feel the worry in the hearts of the people around me. I could tell that when they hugged me they were probably wondering if it would be for the last time. I remember feeling so scared.

After waking up from my ten-hour brain surgery, I completely lost my balance. I had to use a stupid walker. I couldn't even stand up on my own, put on my own pants without sitting down, or hold my babies. I remember Mike driving me home from the hospital, and I was so dizzy that I had to lay flat in the truck, and I felt like I was on the world's biggest rollercoaster, ready to puke at any moment. Losing my balance was one of the most frustrating things that happened to me. I lost all independence, and I was terrified it would never come back.

But a year later, I was able to stand up paddle board again! Shortly after that I went golfing and actually played really well! We took the walker out of storage and donated it to someone in need.

I had come to terms that I would be bald for life but discovered how fun it could be to sport a different look each day. I enjoyed having fun with purple, green, and regular brown wigs and found that hats and scarves were just as cute. Even though there were days I felt confident with my new body, I often still felt sad, missing my long, wavy brown hair. I felt insecure, and I worried about all the weight that prednisone packed onto my body. In one year, my pant size had gone from a size 8, down to a size 0, and back up to a 12. I looked forward to the day when things would level out, and I could have just one size in my closet.

Each day, I felt like I was falling more in love with Mike, if that was even possible. My heart was twitter-patted, like it had been when we started dating at sixteen. We were laughing and joking with each other. I just wanted to be in his arms all the time and was constantly amazed that he was mine. We did normal, everyday things together, like folding laundry and making dinner, and it was fun and exciting. It felt tremendous to finally be thriving again, living our simple dream life together.

Every now and then, a memory would spark, usually not a good one either, and it triggered my anxiety. Or I would have some weird ache in my chest or head and I would start to jump to the worst conclusion. Because my immune system had been wiped during the stem cell transplant, I got sick fairly easily with common colds.

I began thinking a lot about how to use all of this for good—how to teach my children the lessons we learned as we walked through this cancer hell. How to make sure that all the pain that we endured wasn't wasted—that it could be used for good.

After months of being chauffeured around, I was finally able to drive myself to a doctor's appointment and I felt so confident and independent. It was wonderful to have time to myself and the strength to be on my own.

On the way home from the hospital, I stopped to drop off packages, and a lady I had never met came up to me and asked excitedly, "Are you Kaylie?"

I was so confused—but then she told me that Mike had helped her learn to walk again when he worked at the physical therapy clinic by our apartment. She said she had been following my story, praying for me, and had even donated to our GoFundMe account.

With tears in her eyes she told me that she loved my spirit, and that every time she read my blog she learned something. I gave her a huge hug and thanked her for helping us. And then we talked about how amazing Mike is, how lucky I was to have him, and how incredible God was. She told me to call her the crazy redheaded lady. It brought me so much joy to meet her. There have been so many people that have helped us, both in front and behind the scenes, and to meet this stranger, give her a hug and say thank you in person was simply amazing.

I also made so many new, incredible friendships. One of the most meaningful was with a lady I met on Facebook who had also been diagnosed with a lymphoma brain tumor. In the private group we were in, there were only about four out of 1300 members who had brain involvement like we did. We chatted for a couple of weeks, before we realized that we lived fifteen minutes away from each other! We met at her house for tea. I played with her golden doodle, talked about books we loved, and realized that we had so much more in common than cancer. Since then, we have become true and dear friends to one another.

There have been so many experiences where I have felt the right people have been there, at the right time. People who could encourage me, become my friends, or teach me something. Random encounters, such as the one with the redheaded lady or my Facebook friend, showed me that God truly had a plan for me. Worrying about my future was not necessary because I knew that the trust I'd gained for my Savior during all of this was worth everything. I knew that He was guiding me, and it was okay to let go and just let Him lead. Even though I was getting healthier, mentally and physically, I knew that recovery was going to be a long process, if not a lifelong one. I also know that there are always moments where I am human, and I forget to trust God—moments where I worry, fear, and make mistakes. I am never going to be perfect, and that's okay. I learned that when I'm on the ground, He will pick me up with His gentle hands.

I wish that I could get a "get out of jail free" card and never have to go through another trial in my life, but I know that there will always be storms up ahead. I also know that by the Grace of God, Jesus saved me from a tumultuous, dangerous sea, and brought me back to dry, stable land—a land that is full of love, hope, good friends, and wonderful family. To this day, I still have sea legs, but I'm grateful to be back on the safe shore.

CHAPTER TWENTY-FOUR

hugs.

"Now you are the body of Christ, and each one
of you is a part of it."

-1 Corinthians 12:27 NIV

Being on prednisone for the pneumonia I had acquired during my stem cell transplant made sleeping a real challenge. Every night I would toss and turn, so incredibly tired, but my brain wouldn't shut off. While the steroid was very effective in treating my pneumonia, it also gave me awful side effects: insomnia, moon face, weight gain, bloating, achy joints, stomach aches, fatigue, nausea, and horrible headaches. In addition, because of the damaging effects of chemo, my body had gone into premature menopause. Throughout the night, every pore on my body would release sweat, and I would wake up drenched in my sheets.

One night, around three AM, I woke up. My left leg was being difficult and wouldn't settle down, and I was having another hot flash. Mike lay next to me in bed, snoring, sleeping like a baby. It was pouring rain outside, and in that peaceful moment I had time to think. This wasn't the first night I'd spent alone in the quiet hours; but the day's events were flowing through the space in my mind more so than usual.

Earlier that day we had gone to the SCCA Pulmonary Clinic for my Pulmonary Function Test. It was the fifth one I'd had, and each time I'd get a kick out of it. The whole experience was kind of bizarre. They sat me in a glass box room, had me put a huge nose plug on, and breathe into a giant mouth guard attached to all sorts of different tubes. The respiratory therapist who runs it was super enthusiastic and sweet, and encouraged me to "breathe in as deep as you can…a little more…a little more…and POW! Push it all out until you feel like you're going to pass out." On the monitor outside of the glass box, my breath was shown animated as if it was a bowling ball going down a lane towards the pins. I felt like I was playing the Wii bowling game but with my lungs. It was one of the more entertaining tests I'd had, and the good news was, I passed! My lungs were strong and healthy, which meant that soon I would be able to stop taking the steroid meds and would be able to function like a human being again and not some hyped up, overtired insomniac.

Mike and the kids drove me to the clinic because driving downtown Seattle stresses me out. Mike and the kids hung out in the playroom while I did my test. Afterwards I walked past the receptionist who recognized me, smiled, and asked me how I was doing. I didn't think she remembered me, but she did, and it sure touched my heart! I gave her a quick update and then went and poked my head into the playroom to gather my little family.

Tug was tired, and beyond ready for his morning nap. Zoey began her constant chatter, telling me all about the picture she had drawn for me while I had been gone for twenty whole minutes. Mike gave me a hug, and we scooped up Tuggy and stopped at the vending machine for some quick snacks before fighting traffic back home.

We got onto the parking garage elevator, pushing the level C button. Just before the doors closed, a family of three quickly stepped into the elevator with us. I noticed that they looked like they were close to our age. The man was holding a blonde-haired little girl, probably around two, that looked just like her mama standing next to them. As the elevator went slowly down, I looked over at Mike, and he motioned to the family standing in front of us and gave me a sad smile. The mom leaned over on her man's shoulder and began to cry. I looked back at Mike, and I knew exactly what he was thinking.

That was us, just a year before. A small family, the mom just finding out some sort of awful news, a husband comforting his wife while simultaneously breaking inside, and a little girl with no clue what was going on. I watched, feeling so much empathy for them, knowing exactly what they felt even though I knew nothing about them. It was different seeing it from another perspective. To be on the hopeful side of cancer, rather than the side of despair and grief.

The family got off the elevator on level C with us, stopping at a car closer to the elevator entrance. The man gave the girl to the woman, as he backed up their SUV, so they could get in. Mike continued to walk to the car with our kids, but I had this nagging feeling that I needed to go back and talk to her. Mike already knew I was going to, and said, "Go." So, I ran down the rows of cars and tapped her on the shoulder. She turned around with tears and sorrow written all over her face.

I don't know why, but I said, "I don't know your story, but you look like you really need a hug." As we hugged with her little girl on her hip, she wept on my shoulder.

After a few moments, she pulled back and said, "Thank you, thank you so much." I then told her, pointing down the row of cars at my husband holding our son, "I was pregnant when I found out…and I'm in remission now. My baby is over there, and he just turned two. You're going to be okay. You are all going to be okay no matter what happens."

We hugged one more time, and again, she said, "Thank you." Smiling, I looked into her eyes, and said, "Have a good day." I walked back to our car, where Mike and Tug were waiting for me. Tug practically jumped into my arms, and I could see that the woman was looking at us, with a sad smile, but a smile nonetheless. I got into the car, and we left.

On the way home, a memory sparked of someone giving me a hug just when I needed it. It was after my first round of chemotherapy. I was thirty weeks pregnant, Zoey was just barely three years old, and I thought that I would be okay taking myself to my appointment—I wasn't.

After my appointment, I was so shaky and felt completely unwell. Zoey was hungry, and so I hobbled through the cafeteria as she picked out something to eat. She chose some Sun Chips, and I grabbed an apple juice. As I went to pay, I quickly realized I had forgotten my wallet. I pulled Zoey aside and told her, holding back the tears, that I was so sorry, but she would have to wait until we got home.

Just then, this sweet lady came up to us, and said, "I don't know your story, but you look like you really need a hug." As she gave me a hug, my big pregnant belly pressed between us, my little girl holding onto my leg, I wept on her shoulder. She pulled away, smiling and said, "Hand me your treats. I'm paying." Instantly, I broke down sobbing. "Thank you, thank you, thank you," I said. She said, "Don't worry about it sweetheart; we all have bad days. You're going to be okay."

As I lay in my bed thinking about that beautiful woman in the elevator, her gorgeous daughter and protective man, I thought about how important human connection is. I thought about how easy it is to become distracted and not notice those around us, how often everyone is occupied by their screens. What if I had been distracted, and I had missed the chance to give this person a hug?

I thought about it for a long time, about how I was incredibly grateful that after all we'd been through (and still going through), that I am still here—that I am given opportunities to be the arms of Jesus and help comfort those in need; that His Love can be shown through others and through me. We are here on this planet to Love and Be Loved. What a tremendous blessing!

I just gave her a hug. It didn't cost me anything, but it felt so good to my heart to do so.

The lady in the cafeteria gave me a hug and bought our

lunch. She didn't have to do it either; but she saw that I was hurting, and I needed comfort. She was aware and attune to the suffering around her. God bless her.

I can't help but think about how glorious it would be if everyone paid more attention and helped even just a little bit more. One of my favorite sayings is "we are blessed to be a blessing." Wouldn't it be great if we all lived that way?

I thought that once I was in remission, cancer would just be a thing of the past. But I quickly learned that it's going to follow me around my whole life. I can't change anything about what happened to me, but I can choose to learn from it. I know each day I'm still learning—about patience, kindness, and grace. Each day God gives us opportunities to do His work—to be His presence in this world. I pray that I'm mindful enough not to miss the chances to do so.

love.

"We love because He first loved us."

-1 John 4:19 NIV

Cancer tried to ruin my life, and instead it made it more meaningful. My fight was tremendously challenging, but I made it! I am a survivor! Cancer did not destroy me or my spirit. It taught me that I can make it through hell and back, and I won't have to do it alone.

Cancer has also been a blessing. It taught me so much about myself, that I could do really hard things, and that I am stronger than I ever imagined. It showed me that there is kindness all around me, that people step up to the plate to help others in need. It reaffirmed the belief that families are our most treasured possessions.

Most importantly, it gave me insight about the nature of God. He wants us to have joy in our journeys and will create beautiful things out of dust. He is a God who fills us with His love, which we can then pour into others. He is a God who loves so extravagantly that He died for us, rose from the dead, atoning for the sins of the world!

Life is uncertain, and there is a chance cancer could come back. I do worry sometimes, but most of the time, I'm just happy: happy to be alive, taking care of my little ones, playing with my dog, loving my husband. We always seem to be a little short on money, but we have a comfy place to sleep and plenty to eat. Most importantly, we are blessed with incredible friends and family.

I don't know where to go next. For the first time, I've stopped planning every detail of my life because I know that plans never go the way I expect them to—and I'm okay with that. I trust that the plans God has for me will be so much greater than I could ever have made for myself. I know that He will always be there with me, and that is all I need.

Our little family knows that we are loved by our Creator. We also know that everyone on this earth is a child of God, and therefore we should show kindness to one another and love our neighbors.

In the darkest parts of our lives, His light shines the brightest. I feel honored that He allowed our family to be torchbearers for His brilliance. Nothing I have done is something I could have accomplished on my own. The greatest author of all time wrote this story. His grace, His peace, His hope is written all over this world. All we need to do is look for it. There will always be tough chapters in our stories, but we must keep reading, knowing that there is a purpose for it all, and that light will always overcome the darkness.

I'm curious to see what the next chapters in my life will

look like, but I'm content knowing that it will continue to be a good story. I look forward to the time when I can look back and see how everything is woven together, and I'm able to understand the purpose of it all.

Until then, my goal will be to try and make each moment count and to show appreciation always. To help those who are in need. To forgive myself and others when expectations are not met. To worship my God that I love so much. To love others and accept love. And always remember,

Life is a beautiful thing.